FIGHT LIKE A CATHOLIC

Spiritual Warfare *in the* Catholic Tradition

Written by
Susan Brinkmann, OCDS

Foreword by
Fr. Isaac Haywiser, OSB

P.O. Box 1173
Pottstown, PA 19464

Nihil Obstat
Rev. Msgr. Joseph G. Prior
Censor Liborum

Imprimatur
Most Rev. Nelson J. Perez
Archbishop of Philadelphia
June 2020

Copyright ©2020 by Susan Brinkmann

All rights reserved. No part of this publication may be reproduced, distributed or transmitted in any form or by any means, without prior written permission.

Scripture citations used in this work are taken from the Revised Standard Version, ©Oxford University Press, 2008.

Catholic Life Institutes Press
PO Box 1173
Pottstown, PA 19464
www.catholiclifeinstitute.org

Cover Image by Deacon Lawrence Klimecki, www.deaconlawrence.org
Cover Design by IGD Graphic Design, www.image-gd.com
Interior Design by Elizabeth Racine, www.ElizabethRacine.com

Fight Like a Catholic/ Susan Brinkmann—1st ed.
ISBN 978-1-7336724-4-3

"What are the Church's greatest needs
at the present time?
Don't be surprised at our answer,
and don't write it off as simplistic or even superstitious:
one of the Church's greatest needs is to be
defended against the evil we call the Devil."

– Pope St. Paul VI
Confronting the Devil's Power, 1972

TABLE OF CONTENTS

Foreword .... *i*

Introduction 1

Chapter One 13
Who is Satan?

Chapter Two 29
Ordinary Satanic Activity:
Temptation to Acquire Hidden Powers

Chapter Three 55
Ordinary Satanic Activity:
Temptation to Acquire Secret Knowledge

Chapter Four 87
Extraordinary Satanic Activity

Chapter Five 107
How to Combat Satan

APPENDIX A 127
Protecting Oneself and the Home from Evil

APPENDIX B 143
Bibliography

FOREWORD

Growing up as a child in the 1990s included watching Batman, Superman, Spiderman, the X-Men, Power Rangers and various other superhero shows. I was also exposed early on to the lives of the Saints, particularly in a book of saints that I had for years. I likewise enjoyed the Biblical stories of such heroes as David, Daniel, and others. Heroes attract us because they challenge us to go beyond what we think is possible. Unfortunately, we can also come to the conclusion that we are unable to do what they do, particularly if their powers seem beyond natural. We recognize our human condition following the Fall of Adam and Eve, the inherent weakness of Original Sin that, although removed through Baptism, is still a part of our lives through concupiscence, that tendency toward sin. As Christians, as Catholics, we are baptized into battle, we are called to be heroes after the Hero, Jesus Christ.

We hear this call in the Scriptures: in the Garden of Eden, God tells Satan, the devil, in Genesis 3:15, *"I will put enmity between you and the woman, and between your seed and her seed; he shall bruise your head, and you shall bruise his heel."*[1] While we recognize that this is fulfilled in Mary and our Lord Jesus Christ as the New Eve and New Adam, respectively, we also recognize that this is our battle as well. In the book of Revelation 12:7 17 we read:

> Now war arose in heaven, Michael and his angels fighting against the dragon; and the dragon and his angels fought, but they were defeated and there was no longer any place for them in heaven. And the great dragon was thrown

---

[1] Catholic Biblical Association (Great Britain). (1994). The Holy Bible: Revised Standard Version, Catholic Edition (Ge 3:15). New York: National Council of Churches of Christ in the USA. (Hereafter RSVCE).

down, that ancient serpent, who is called the Devil and Satan, the deceiver of the whole world—he was thrown down to the earth, and his angels were thrown down with him. And I heard a loud voice in heaven, saying, "Now the salvation and the power and the kingdom of our God and the authority of his Christ have come, for the accuser of our brethren has been thrown down, who accuses them day and night before our God. And they have conquered him by the blood of the Lamb and by the word of their testimony, for they loved not their lives even unto death. Rejoice then, O heaven and you that dwell therein! But woe to you, O earth and sea, for the devil has come down to you in great wrath, because he knows that his time is short!"

And when the dragon saw that he had been thrown down to the earth, he pursued the woman who had borne the male child. But the woman was given the two wings of the great eagle that she might fly from the serpent into the wilderness, to the place where she is to be nourished for a time, and times, and half a time. The serpent poured water like a river out of his mouth after the woman, to sweep her away with the flood. But the earth came to the help of the woman, and the earth opened its mouth and swallowed the river which the dragon had poured from his mouth. Then the dragon was angry with the woman, and went off to make war on the rest of her offspring, on those who keep the commandments of God and bear testimony to Jesus. And he stood on the sand of the sea.[2]

As you reflect on this passage, note that Satan is cast to the earth, not hell, to make war with the children of God. Rightly, then, does St. Peter tell us in chapter 5:8-9, "Be sober, be watchful. Your adversary the devil prowls around like a roaring lion, seeking some one to devour. Resist him, firm in your faith, knowing that the same experience of suffering is required of your

---

2 Ibid

brotherhood throughout the world."³ The battle begun in Eden continues to today, though now we have the gift of the Holy Spirit and the graces won for us on the cross by our Lord Jesus Christ.

As those baptized children of God, we are given the armor we need, as St. Paul reminds us in Ephesians 6:10 and following. This requires us to turn from all idolatry, as St. Paul warns us in 1Corinthians 10:14-22. It is to these realities that this book calls our attention and that Susan Brinkmann, through her extensive research, helps us to understand. This book is a timely work for all our consideration as the realities of spiritual warfare increase and the battle intensifies in our own day and age.

What does this battle look like today? This is a great question and one that we all need to think about seriously. Whether we are aware of these realities or not, we see them through various means of communication, most notably the television and streamed shows. We observe Satan subtly tricking us through our everyday temptations, but I also see his tactics through, for example, Disney's *Descendants* movies, which, though seeking to show that everyone is not bound to evil and has the possibility for change, a good quality, it does not call for a complete conversion and turning away from evil. Rather, these movies attribute the evil done by the villainous parents and their children as the result of a misunderstanding that can be easily forgiven, rather than calling them to turn away from a deliberate decision and acceptance of the consequences of that decision, such as accepting a form of penance. This is an attack on objective, universal Truth and the accompanying realities.

More explicitly I see this through the FreeForm Channel's *31 Nights of Halloween* in October, through the endless fascination with the undead, zombies, werewolves, etc. – Twilight series anyone? – and through more shows that seek to downplay evil as innocent or somehow good or misunderstood. This relativizing of evil is best expressed through the COEXIST bumper sticker since society claims that our fighting in this world is all just

---

3 Ibid

one big misunderstanding, everyone is accepted, all behavior is acceptable if no one is getting hurt, and so all need to just get along. This extends even to the call for Satanism to be accepted as a religion protected by the Constitution and even have a statue of Satan erected in state capitals. While I am all for peace and cooperation among humanity, Satan does not get a vote in this matter, nor is he to have a place in society since he is the one who seeks our destruction, not our ultimate good. Only through Jesus Christ and His Church, following His commands and example of love, is any of this truly possible. Our trust in Him is being attacked in these battles.

I see the battle happening also when I stop at such events like the local Renaissance Fair and how magic has crept back into an acceptable place in society. Take for instance the Harry Potter series books and movies, which I have read and seen. It's a good story, well written and about great things such as friendship and the value of working through life's challenges with the support of others. On the other hand, it has become a vehicle for increased illusions that magic exists, that we can control life and nature, and all we need is a bit of luck. Couple this with our society's increasing desire to be free of God and this does not exactly foster growth in the Christian trust in God's Divine Providence.

Better yet, back to the superhero shows, I have also seen almost all the latest superhero movies. In these we see and hear that magic is equated with science not explained. Superheroes are great, but they are also debilitating. You and I, as Catholic Christians, have been given all that we need to fight Satan, to overcome temptations, to live a virtuous life, much like those we idolize in society today. The challenge that we have to acknowledge is that they are not Jesus Christ, and He calls us to something far greater – love, self-sacrificial love. I have seen printed on a t-shirt an image of Jesus sitting with superheroes telling them that He saved the world in one day and it raised the question in my mind - what have these current idols done? Are not their stories simply fantasy while the story of Jesus Christ is more real than any book we can read or any movies we can see? It is! Thank God! We likewise must recognize that the battle is real and the victory is ours in Jesus Christ, we only have to willingly engage in that battle.

So, I invite you to read this little book. Get ready for the adventure and the battles that are contained within life. Armor up! As we read in Ephesians 6:10-20:

> Finally, be strong in the Lord and in the strength of his might. Put on the whole armor of God, that you may be able to stand against the wiles of the devil. For we are not contending against flesh and blood, but against the principalities, against the powers, against the world rulers of this present darkness, against the spiritual hosts of wickedness in the heavenly places. Therefore take the whole armor of God, that you may be able to withstand in the evil day, and having done all, to stand. Stand therefore, having girded your loins with truth, and having put on the breastplate of righteousness, and having shod your feet with the equipment of the gospel of peace; besides all these, taking the shield of faith, with which you can quench all the flaming darts of the evil one. And take the helmet of salvation, and the sword of the Spirit, which is the word of God. Pray at all times in the Spirit, with all prayer and supplication. To that end keep alert with all perseverance, making supplication for all the saints, and also for me, that utterance may be given me in opening my mouth boldly to proclaim the mystery of the gospel, for which I am an ambassador in chains; that I may declare it boldly, as I ought to speak. [4]

Find strength in the battle: seek spiritual direction. Use the weapons of the Church's armory: the rosary, novenas, fasting and other such tactics. God has given us free will to choose to follow Him and return His gift of love. In this relationship He gives us opportunities to grow in love. With God's permission Satan tempts us and seeks to trip us up. DO NOT BE AFRAID!! Know what is going on – avoid idolatry, even if you are doing something "just for fun" – do not open the door to Satan but to

---
[4] Ibid

Christ. Listen to His most Sacred Heart. As my Holy Father Saint Benedict wrote in the Prologue to his *Rule*:

> Listen, O my son, to the teachings of your master, and turn to them with the ear of your heart. Willingly accept the advice of a devoted father and put it into action. Thus you will return by the labor of obedience to the one from whom you drifted through the inertia of disobedience. Now then I address my words to you: whoever is willing to renounce self-will, and take up the powerful and shining weapons of obedience to fight for the Lord Christ, the true king.[5]

We are called to fight for the true King! I pray that Susan's book will help you in this battle.

May you know the Love of the Father, the grace of the Son and the power of the Holy Spirit. May our Blessed Mother watch over you and guard you as only a mother can.

May you know the protection of St. Michael and your guardian angel.

May Saint Benedict help you to fight well and overcome the inertia of disobedience.

May God bless you and keep you ever in His loving care, not giving you anything that you cannot handle without His grace working in you.

Psalm 125: A Song of Ascents.

> Those who trust in the Lord are like Mount Zion, which cannot be moved, but abides for ever. As the mountains are round about Jerusalem, so the Lord is round about his people, from this time forth and for evermore. For the scepter of wickedness shall not rest upon the land allotted

---

[5] Kardong, T. (1999). *Benedict's Rule: a Translation* (electronic edition., pp. 3–4). Collegeville, MN: The Liturgical Press.

> to the righteous, lest the righteous put forth their hands to do wrong. Do good, O Lord, to those who are good, and to those who are upright in their hearts! But those who turn aside upon their crooked ways the Lord will lead away with evildoers! Peace be in Israel! [6]

Psalm 121: A Song of Ascents.

> I lift up my eyes to the hills. From whence does my help come? My help comes from the Lord, who made heaven and earth. He will not let your foot be moved, he who keeps you will not slumber. Behold, he who keeps Israel will neither slumber nor sleep. The Lord is your keeper; the Lord is your shade on your right hand. The sun shall not smite you by day, nor the moon by night. The Lord will keep you from all evil; he will keep your life. The Lord will keep your going out and your coming in from this time forth and for evermore.[7]

Ut in omnibus glorificetur Deus,

Fr. Isaac Haywiser, O.S.B.
Benedictine Monk
Saint Vincent Archabbey
April 23, 2020

The Memorial of		
Saint Adalbert of Prague	&	Saint George
Bishop, Martyr		Martyr
d. April 23, 997		d. c. April 23, 303

---

6 RSVCE
7 Ibid

Introduction

"We must fight against spirits, the spirits that swarm all around us. In other words, we must fight against the demon... Why do we not speak about it anymore?"
— Pope St. Paul VI

On June 29, 1972, Pope Paul VI gave a speech so controversial that it nearly sparked an international scandal. What was it about?

The devil.

Instead of carefully considering what the pontiff had to say, journalists scoffed at the whole idea of the devil and accused the pope of being stuck in the Dark Ages. No one believed in the devil anymore, they claimed, at least no one except the backward people who still go to church on Sunday.

What the media didn't realize then, and still don't to this day, is that these comments do little more than reveal their own incredible illiteracy about a subject that affects all of humanity regardless of whether or not we believe it's true.

As the late great Roman exorcist, Father Gabriele Amorth quipped: "In their ignorance, they did not realize that we go back farther than that [the Dark Ages]: to the Gospel, to biblical history, to Adam and Eve!"[8]

---

8 Amorth, Father Gabriele, *An Exorcist: More Stories* (San Francisco, CA; *Ignatius Press*, 2002) pg. 64

Regardless of their mockery, the Pope would not be silenced. A few months later, on November 15, 1972, he expanded on the same subject in a general audience, portions of which will be reproduced throughout this study. He began his speech by expounding upon why he believed people dismissed the subject of the devil.

"Why do we not speak about it anymore? We do not speak about it because we lack a visible experience. We believe that what we do not see does not exist. Instead, we fight against evil. But, what is evil? We are speaking of evil as a deficiency, a lack of something. If someone is ill, he lacks health. If someone is poor, he lacks money. And so on. This is not the case when we speak about the devil; that is why this is a terrible reality. We are not dealing with a deficiency, an evil caused by the lack of something. We must realize that we face an efficiency that is evil in itself; an existing evil, an evil that is a person; an evil that we cannot classify as corruption of goodness. We are speaking of an affirmation of evil, and if this does not frighten us, it should."[9]

Our Holy Father stated emphatically that "anyone who refuses to acknowledge the existence of this terrible reality departs from the truth of biblical and ecclesiastical teaching."[10]

It seems hard to believe that even in the face of this clear and precise warning, along with thousands of years of teaching on the existence of Satan, there are so many Catholics today who refuse to believe in his existence.

According to the Applied Center for Research in the Apostolate (CARA) at Georgetown University, belief in the devil has actually risen in recent years, from 62 percent in 1957 to 70 percent in 2007. However, just as Pope Paul explained, the majority don't believe he's actually a personal being.

"For many, the devil or Satan is a symbol of evil rather than a being ... Among the 85% of U.S. adults who believe in God that were asked the question, 69% see Satan more as a symbol of

---
9 Ibid, pg. 65
10 Ibid

evil and 31% say they believe Satan is a 'living being.' Evangelical Christians are among the most likely to believe Satan is a being (55%). Catholics are among the least likely to agree (17%). Eighty-three percent of Catholics say they see Satan more as a symbol of evil."[11]

As disturbing as these statistics might be, they're hardly surprising. Disbelief in the devil has insinuated even the highest echelons of the Church. For example, in 2019, during an interview with the Italian magazine, *Tempi*, Father Arturo Sosa, SJ, the Superior General of the Society of Jesus, declared that the devil was a symbol, not a person.

The devil, "exists as the personification of evil in different structures, but not in persons, because [it] is not a person, [it] is a way of acting evil. He is not a person like a human person. It is a way of evil to be present in human life," Fr. Sosa said. "Good and evil are in a permanent war in the human conscience and we have ways to point them out. We recognize God as good, fully good. Symbols are part of reality, and the devil exists as a symbolic reality, not as a personal reality."[12]

His remarks sparked an international controversy, with his statement repeated in headlines throughout the Christian and secular media only to be partially walked back a few months later when Fr. Sosa told Italian journalists that "the power of the devil... obviously still exists as a force that tries to ruin our efforts."[13]

By then, the damage had been done, and those Catholics who were already doubting the existence of the devil had one more excuse to continue to dismiss the reality of Satan.

Decades earlier, Pope Paul may have been addressing these same doubters when he insisted: "What I am telling you is

---

[11] "A New Age Old Scratch?" *1964 Blog*, Applied Center for Research into the Apostolate, August 24, 2017
[12] "Jesuit Superior General: Satan is a 'Symbolic Reality,'" *Catholic News Agency*, August 21, 2019
[13] "Jesuit Superior General: Satan is Real and Wants us to Reject God," *Catholic News Agency*, December 6, 2019

not my delusion, nor am I encouraging you to be superstitious. I am simply telling you that this reality exists. I repeat, the Gospel speaks to us about it on many, many pages. That is why it is important that we perceive evil. We must have a correct, Christian conception of the world, of life, of salvation."[14]

But those doubts persisted, even to the point where some wondered if there should be a "revision of doctrine" on the whole subject of Satan, beginning with Scripture.

"Some critics, believing they can define Jesus' own position, claim that none of his words guarantees demonic reality," we read in the Church document, *Christian Faith and Demonology*. It was just a reflection of the beliefs of His time.

"They assert that affirmation of the existence of this reality, where it is made, rather reflects the ideas of Jewish writings, or is dependent on New Testament traditions, but not on Christ. Since it does not form part of the central Gospel message, the existence of demonic reality, they say, no longer has a call on our faith today, and we are free to reject it."[15]

Those who make these assertions are doing so on unconvincing evidence, especially where the New Testament is concerned. In these pages we find that Jesus, who was characterized by his independence of spirit with regard to the opinions of His time, didn't just believe in Satan because this was the compelling belief of the time. In fact, in the Acts of the Apostles, the Sadducees admit "neither resurrection nor angel, nor spirit."[16] This means that they didn't believe in either angels or devils, so opinion on the existence of Satan was very much unsettled at the time of Christ.

"There is no disputing the fact that Christ, and even more so the apostles, belonged to their times and shared the current culture. Nevertheless, because of his divine nature and the

---

14 *An Exorcist: More Stories*, pg. 66
15 *Christian Faith and Demonology* (Boston, MA; *Pauline Books & Media*), pg. 7-8
16 Acts 23:8

revelation which he had come to communicate, Jesus transcended his milieu and his times; he was immune to their pressure ... So, to assert today that Jesus' discourse on Satan was only a borrowed doctrine without importance for universal belief, seems, even at first sight, to be an ill-informed opinion on the times and on the personality of the Master."[17]

Jesus' personal witness is, in itself, a powerful indicator of the existence of Satan.

In addition to his temptation in the dessert, and his frequent casting out of devils, he also spoke about the devil in his parables, such as when he attributed to Satan the cockles spread in the field (Matt 13:25); when he warned Peter that the "powers of death" would try to prevail against the Church and try to sift him like wheat (Luke 22:31); when he left the Upper Room on the night of his death and declared the arrival of the "prince of this world" (John 14:30); when the soldiers laid hands on him in the Garden of Gethsemane and he declared that the "reign of darkness" had come (Luke 22:53).

"These facts and these declarations – which are well placed, repeated, and in harmony with one another – are the result of change. They cannot be treated as fables to be demythologized. Otherwise, one would have to admit that in those critical hours the mind of Jesus, whose lucidity and self-control before the judges are attested to by the Scripture accounts, was a prey to illusory fantasies and that his word was devoid of all firmness. This would be in contradiction to the impression of the first hearers and of the present readers of the Gospel."[18]

As a result of these ideas being promulgated by the learned and spread in prestigious journals, the faithful are left confused. "The faithful, accustomed to take seriously the warning of Christ and of the apostolic writings, feel that this kind of teaching is meant to influence opinion."[19]

---

17 *Christian Faith and Demonology*, pg.10
18 *Christian Faith and Demonology*, pg. 12
19 Ibid

Of course, this is precisely what Satan desires. As Venerable Fulton J. Sheen explained in his book *Life of Christ,* "Very few people believe in the devil these days, which suits the devil very well. He is always helping to circulate the news of his own death. The essence of God is existence, and He defines Himself as: 'I am Who am.' The essence of the devil is the lie, and he defines himself as: 'I am who am not.' Satan has very little trouble with those who do not believe in him; they are already on his side."[20]

This situation is only exacerbated in our post-Christian culture by the distortions of Satan being promulgated by the popular entertainment industry. With the exception of a few films that portrayed the devil and exorcism in realistic terms, such as William Friedkin's, *The Exorcist* (1973), and James Wan's *The Conjuring* (2013), Hollywood's idea of Satan seems to be based more on politics than reality.

"The themes portrayed are consistent: malevolent supernatural forces are real, humans are powerless in the face of evil, Christian doctrine and religious training provide no recourse or significant spiritual guidance in the struggle with evil, and the Christian Church and its leaders are powerless before Satan and his minions. In addition, God is too distant, or uncaring, unable, or unwilling, to check Satan's power," explains Baptist minister John Ankerberg.

"These films, and others like them, borrow freely from Christian teachings and symbols, but usually subvert them beyond recognition or take such dramatic license that any sound theological insight is lost. They often purport to quote from the Bible or to interpret biblical eschatology, but these interpretations are horribly skewed at best. Several of the movies are visually stunning in their special effects so, even if one is able to recognize the faulty theology, the world they portray is so compelling that it is hard not to accept Hollywood's version as true. Thus it is not surprising that many ... are unable to distinguish the unorthodox

---

20 Sheen, Rev. Fulton J., *Life of Christ* (Mansfield Centre, CT: *Martino Publishing,* 2016)

teaching in these films. Instead, they come away convinced they have learned something valuable about Christianity and its inability to deal with evil."[21]

The prevalence of occult-based fiction is another area where the devil is happily concealing his activity beneath distorted portrayals of occult activities, particularly that of sorcery which are found in popular book series such as *Harry Potter, Goosebumps, The Kane Chronicles*, and the Jane Madison series on witchcraft which is a bestseller among teen girls.

"...The young readers are taken into a world where everything is possible through witchcraft," writes German sociologist Gabriele Kuby. "The experience of powerlessness in the real world of everyday life is relieved through the fantastic experience of magical power. The tight rules of human life are deactivated. Every situation can change at any moment through curse and anti-curse, through magic and anti-magic, in any direction. Everything is allowed which serves one's own interests, the limit is only the greater power of the other person."[22]

Even video games have been infiltrated by occult themes that make the devil into a kind of superhero. In the game *Tecmo's Deception: Invitation to Darkness*, which is rated for teens, players make an unholy pact and sell their soul to the devil with the object of the game being to ensure the resurrection of Satan and to obtain his power. Some of the most popular games such as *Doom, World of Warcraft*, and *Mortal Kombat* make liberal use of satanic themes and/or imagery.

The demonic is also infiltrating the world of children's games. The ever-popular Ouija board makes no effort to hide what it's about. Manufactured by Hasbro Games, it taunts: "Gather around the board, if you dare, and unlock secrets from a mysterious and mystifying world. You have questions, and the spirit world has answers – and the uncanny Ouija board is your

---
21 "How Hollywood is Rewriting the Way We See God, the Devil, and Ourselves," *The John Ankerberg Show*, 2001
22 Kuby, Gabriele, quoted by Michael D. O'Brien in *Harry Potter and the Paganization of Culture*, (Rzeszow, Poland: *Fides et Traditio Press*, 2010) pg 61

way to get them. What do you want to know? Grab a friend and ask the board a question, using the included planchette, but be patient and concentrate because the spirits can't be rushed. Handle the Ouija board with respect, and it won't disappoint you!"[23]

In the game, *Magic: The Gathering*, players role-play as sorcerers and use trading cards that are linked to five different kinds of magic to destroy their opponents through the use of spells and enchantments.

Lest we think occult-themed play is just for children, it's important to note that adults have been at it for centuries with the use of tarot, astrology, and other "parlor room games" such as seances and visits to mediums who are more than happy to conjure who they believe to be spirits of the dead.

The combination of these entertainment trends that relegate Satan to the realm of amusement, along with the cultural decline in religious adherence and headlines such as those generated by Father Sosa about the devil being just a symbol, have all converged to produce a frightening ambivalence among the faithful in regard to the reality of evil.

This condition is only worsened by a prevailing relativism and its quest for social "tolerance."

As Father Michael Scanlon explains, "... [M]odern Western culture puts a very high premium on such things as mutual understanding, dialogue, compromise, and individual expression. These are based on a concept of pluralism which insures that everyone can do what they want and think as they please. What is important is not that there be agreement about things but that we understand where each is 'coming from.'"[24]

While dialogue, compromise, and tolerance are important aspects of life, Western society has divinized them, Father Scanlon says. "The result is a myopic view of life which holds that everyone

---

23 Ouija Board Game, Hasbro Gaming, accessed on Amazon
24 Scanlon, Michael TOR, and Randall J. Cirner, *Deliverance from Evil Spirits: A Weapon for Spiritual Warfare* (Ann Arbor, MI: *Servant Books*, 1980) pg. 25-26

– indeed reality itself – must be cooperative and tolerant. Thus the concept of an evil entity bent on one's total destruction doesn't find much room in Western thinking. The concept gets dismissed as lacking in logic, propriety, and the 'modern way.' Because Western man has decided that malevolent forces shouldn't exist he concludes that they actually do not exist."[25]

With the preachers offering little to counter these trends, Christians are getting most of their information from Hollywood and the surrounding culture which leaves them bereft of the factual knowledge they need in order to engage the enemy they are obligated to fight by virtue of their Baptism. Few are even aware of what is meant by spiritual warfare, let alone how to effectively wage it. And yet, it is a reality all Christians must face – whether they believe it or not.

As Catholic author John Labriola writes, "When you were born, you were born into a war zone. When you were baptized, you were fitted with combat boots. You also, in that precise moment, became a redeemed child of God and an enemy of Satan. Your baptism, which set you apart for God, set you apart from Satan. The stain of original sin, the enemy's camouflage, is wiped away. In baptism, God, the author of life has cleansed your soul. After baptism, Satan, the hater of life, wants to stain your soul and steal your birthright...Welcome to the Church Militant."[26]

Today's Christian is in dire need of a refresher course on the kingdom of God and the warfare into which they've been born in order to understand and ultimately triumph in the battle against evil. They need to understand that "The New Testament proclamation of the kingdom of God and the realities inherent in that proclamation utterly destroy the foundations for the bland Christianity so often preached today," warns Father Michael Scanlan. "The forcefulness and the violence with which Jesus confronted all that opposed the kingdom of God belies any notion that the Christian life is one of ease. In fact, Jesus tells his disciples

---

25 Ibid
26 Labriola, John, *Onward Catholic Soldier* (*Luke 1:38 Publishing*: 2008) pg. 17

that they can expect the same kind of life he himself had as they preach the kingdom (MK 10:24-25)."[27]

A review of the four main principles comprising the biblical proclamation of the Kingdom of God would be an invaluable exercise for modern Christians. These principles are: 1) that the reign of God has come into the world in the presence of Jesus; 2) that all men can and must enter the kingdom of God in order to be saved; 3) that the kingdom of God is destroying the kingdom of Satan, and; 4) the kingdom of God will be fully established and the kingdom of Satan eternally destroyed at the second coming of the Lord Jesus Christ.[28]

We can't really say that there are "two kingdoms" – the kingdom of God and the kingdom of Satan – because Satan is not a god or a spiritual force that is capable of independent activity. "Satan is a creature of God and is subject to God's restraints in every way except that he possesses free will."[29]

"At the same time, however, the scriptures do clearly talk about the kingdom of Satan which is antagonistic toward God's Kingdom (Mt 12:25-28)," Father Scanlan explains. "Satan's kingdom is the kingdom of this world (Lk 4:5-6). In his enmity toward God, the ruler of this kingdom, wants to stifle the life of the kingdom of God growing within men. Satan does so through his own personal activity in the hearts of men (Mt. 13:19), and also through the people, ideas, and events which make up the kingdom of this age (Mt. 13:22)."[30]

Whether we realize it or not, all of human society that has become alienated from God due to sin "is in the power of the evil one"[31] which is why Satan is referred to as "the ruler of this world"[32] and even the "god of this world."[33]

---

27 *Deliverance from Evil Spirits*, pg. 5
28 Ibid
29 Ibid, pg. 7
30 *Deliverance from Evil Spirits*, pg. 8
31 1 John 5:19
32 John 16:11
33 2 Cor 4:4

"These texts do not mean the world is under the full control of Satan, since God is also at work in the world and he alone has ultimate sovereignty, but rather that every part of earthly reality is in some way touched by Satan. Satan is not a god in the literal sense; he is only a fallen angel, a creature totally subject to God's restraints (cf. 2 Peter 2:4; Rev 12:7-10). But human beings have placed themselves under this dominion through sin (cf. Jn 8:34). Satan exerts his influence through demons, lesser evil spirits who operate under his rule[34] and also through human beings[35] or the structure of human society.[36] His kingdom is the kingdom of the world."[37]

These two kingdoms exist side-by-side and while waiting for the full realization of the kingdom of God, we must face the reality of evil that abounds in the world. Even though we know that its power has been broken through Jesus Christ, sin, sickness and death still continue to affect us.

"The ruler of this world knows clearly his ultimate ruin is assured. Yet his struggle continues. He wants to sweep to destruction as much as he can before his power is forever taken from him (Rev. 20:10). The devil continues to rule over the world of men opposed to God. He rules those how do not know the good news of the kingdom, and those who do know it but refuse to accept it (1 Jn 5:19). Those who are not in the kingdom of God are surely the easier prey for Satan, but he directs his special wrath against children of the kingdom (Rev. 12:17)... But because we live between the proclamation of the kingdom and its final completion, we must be careful how we live. This fact – that we live between the initial coming of the kingdom of God and its full and final establishment – brings us to the heart of spiritual warfare."[38]

---

34 Matt 9:34
35 John 13:2
36 Ephesians 2:2
37 Luke 4:5-6; Rev 11:15
38 *Deliverance from Evil Spirits*, pg. 9

Before His ascension, Jesus gave us the great commission, to "Go therefore and make disciples of all nations, baptizing them in the name of the Father, and of the Son, and of the Holy Spirit, teaching them to observe all that I have commanded you."[39]

Jesus commanded us to not only proclaim the gospel, but to do so with love for one another. Satan's strategy is aimed at preventing both of these commissions, employing a two-fold strategy: "to keep man in bondage to sin and to the world, thus keeping them from the kingdom of God entirely, and to render ineffective, in any way possible, those who are already in God's kingdom."[40]

God's desire is that we receive his love, forgiveness and abundant life by becoming a member of his family. Satan's desire is that we live in bondage to Satan through bondage to the world and sin, a bondage that will ultimately lead to eternal death in Hell.

"These two purposes are completely inimical to one another. There is no room for compromise, no basis for peaceful coexistence. There can be only struggle and opposition."[41]

Therefore, the Christian must realize that there is no such thing as a cushy life in Christ.

"We live in an interim period between the mortal blow dealt to Satan by the cross and the final destruction of his kingdom when the Lord comes again. During this interim period, God calls his people to attack the kingdom of darkness and to future the kingdom of light. Man is born into the midst of this struggle; by its very nature he *must* fight in it. No one can escape from it. Every man and woman must choose whom they will serve."[42]

---

[39] Matt 28: 19-20
[40] *Deliverance from Evil Spirits*, pg. 10
[41] Ibid, pg. 11
[42] *Deliverance from Evil Spirits*, pg. 11

Chapter One

Who is Satan?

"What I am telling is not my delusion, nor am I encouraging you to be superstitious. I am simply telling you that this reality exists...That is why it is important that we perceive evil. We must have a correct, Christian conception of the world, of life, of salvation."

– *Pope St. Paul VI*

"Non serviam!" ("I will not serve!")

There are no better words to describe the character of Satan than these. He was an angel created by God to be preternaturally good but, by his own doing, chose to reject God and refused to serve him. This decision caused a precipitous drop from the stellar heights of his once pristine goodness and beauty to the depths of all that is evil and hideous.

In order to fully understand *who* he is, and why Satan is so formidable an adversary, we must first consider *what* he is.

Satan is an Angel

One of the most salient – and grossly overlooked – facts about Satan is that he is an angelic being and is thus possessed of preternatural powers that defy human comprehension. Although some of these powers were corrupted by his fall from grace, he is still enormously powerful and dangerous.

Fortunately, we have a wealth of credible sources about the characteristics of preternatural beings which can help to inform us about the capabilities of both the good angels and those who are pitted against us.

One must be careful not think that the information to follow is the stuff of fantasy. As Dr. Peter Kreeft explains, "Angelology is a science, though not an empirical science. It uses an essentially scientific method: gathering data and formulating theories to explain the data. The theories are controlled by the data."[43]

Dr. Kreeft gathers most of his information from the Bible, human experience, and St. Thomas Aquinas who is also known as the "Angelic Doctor" because he wrote the most definitive treatise on angels in the *Summa Theologica*.

It is from these sources that we know angels to be pure spirits, incorporeal substances; free and independent from any material or ethereal body.

As Father Pascal Parente teaches us: "Both his existence and operation are free and independent from matter; nor is the Angel related to a body, like the human soul, which even though perfectly spiritual, is naturally related to the human body as an essential part of the whole human nature. The Angelic nature is wholly spiritual, man's nature is composed of body and spirit."[44]

Scripture tells us that angels, being wholly spiritual, occupy the first and highest place in the scale of created things with man in second place. "Thou hast made him a little less than the Angels."[45]

Every angel is a distinct being having a rational nature with intelligence and liberty. He is considered to be a personal being, and to have an individual personality, such as the affable angel Raphael

---

43 Kreeft, Peter, *Angels (and Demons): What do we really know about them?* (San Francisco, CA: *Ignatius Press*, 1995) pg. 7
44 Parente, Fr. Pascal P., *The Angels: The Catholic Teaching on the Angels* (Rockford, IL: *Tan Books and Publishers*, Inc., 1961) pg. 20-21
45 Psalm 8:6

who guided Tobias on his journeys in the Book of Tobit and the gentle Gabriel who appeared to the Virgin Mary in the Gospel accounts. This is why, Pope Pius XII condemned the opinion of some who 'question whether Angels are personal beings.'"[46]

Even more astonishing is the fact that in addition to every Angel being a personal being, St. Thomas teaches that they differ from one another in so specific a way that "we may say that there are no two Angels of the same species; each of them is his own kind."[47] The number of angels is unknown but is believed to be beyond human calculation. Consider how this compares to the 8.7 million species that currently inhabit the earth.

The intelligence of these beings is also beyond our understanding. Commonly referred to by theologians and philosophers as "minds" or "intelligences," the exalted knowledge and intelligence of the angels is their most outstanding quality.

As Father Parente explains, "Our human mind comes into possession of knowledge by a gradual and laborious process. It requires first of all a number of years of physical development for the proper operation…The Angelic intellect, entirely free and independent from matter and senses needs no such development. It is in the full possession of its power from the very beginning of its existence. There is no need of gathering elements of knowledge bit by bit, of adding ideas to ideas in order to discover truth, as is the case with us. Having been created in the full perfection of its nature, the Angelic mind neither develops by gradual growth nor does it suffer any decay."[48]

In other words, while the human intellect acquires its knowledge little by little, the Angel knows it all at once. They need only to look at something to instantly know everything about it.

Some wonder how Angels can communicate with one another if they have no material body with which to speak. However, we know from Scripture that Angels do indeed talk

---

46 *The Angels*, pg. 26
47 Ibid
48 Ibid, pg. 29

when it is necessary, such as when Gabriel spoke to Zachariah and Mary. But how do they speak to one another?

"St. Thomas holds that Angels talk to each other by a mere act of the will, opening their mind and revealing whatever ideas they wish to convey to others of the same nature as themselves. This Angelic language or conversation, is called illumination."[49]

Although humans must struggle to express themselves, the Angelic language poses no such inhibitions and, as a result, are able to communicate much more precisely.

"To be able to open one's mind and reveal the whole thought, as it is there, without the channel of symbolism, sound, and words, is a higher and better form of expression. Such is the wordless exchanges of ideas, the language of the Angels."[50]

When it comes to angelic movement, it's important to understand that because an Angel is a wholly spiritual being, he doesn't occupy any space so his presence and movements are determined by his activity, such as when the Angel stirred the waters in the pool of Bethsaida.[51]

They move from place to place with what is believed to be the speed of thought.

"Their motion is not really a locomotion but merely an instantaneous change of place, even when the local distance between the second place and the first is of several thousand miles...What a man can do mentally only, an Angel can do by actually transferring his own self and all his activity from one continent to another with the speed of lightning, or better, the speed of thought."[52]

The best evidence we have of this amazing capability is the story of the prophet Habacuc[53] who was on his way to

---

49 *The Angels*, pg. 32
50 Ibid, pg. 33
51 John 5:4
52 *The Angels*, pg 38
53 Daniel 14:32-38

delivering pottage to feed his field workers when an Angel told him to bring the food to Daniel who was languishing in the lion's den in Babylon, which was 600 miles away. "The Angel of the Lord took him by the top of his head and carried him by the hair of his head and set him in Babylon over the den in the force of his spirit."[54] After Daniel had eaten, "the Angel of the Lord presently set Habacuc again in his own place."[55]

As Father Parente explains, Scripture does not tell us that Habacuc was carried "all the way back" to his home, but that he was "set" in his home which was 600 miles away. This implies that the travel was instantaneous.

As for the strength of the Angels, Scripture gives us ample evidence of the super-human capabilities of these creatures, such as when a lone Angel wiped out a whole army of Assyrian warriors in one night.[56] We also read in the Book of Exodus about the incredible plagues that assailed Egypt in the days of Moses, and how, at God's command, the Angels slew the first-born of man and beast.[57]

While some might call these feats "miracles," it's important to note that Angels cannot perform miracles because they are created beings. As St. Thomas explains in the *Summa*, a miracle is "something done by God outside the order of all created nature."[58]

God does, however, frequently commission His Angels to enact His miracles.

Angels are also capable of loving and exercising free will. We know this from the fact that some angels turned against God while others remained faithful.

"Sin cannot exist where there is no free will. Since the Scripture explicitly reveals the sin of the Angels, and their

---

54 Daniel 14:36
55 Daniel 14:38
56 2 Kings 19:35
57 Exodus 11:5
58 Quoted in *The Angels,* pg. 40

banishment from heaven, it clearly implies that they are in possession of a free will."[59]

We also know that the most beautiful and noble act of the Angels is their love. They love God and each other as well as man because man was created in the image of God, was redeemed by the Son of God, and is destined to live with the angels in heaven.

"Yes, the good angels love man as much as Satan hates him."[60]

Although we do not know the exact number of Angels who were created by God, it is generally believed that these spectacular beings are arranged in the nine choirs which are mentioned in Scripture: Seraphim, Cherubim, Thrones, Dominations, Principalities, Powers, Virtues, Archangels, and Angels.

"The mere fact that Scripture carefully distinguishes between these various names of Angelic orders is sufficient reason to believe that they actually represent different ranks in the spirit world, with a difference of perfection and of office between the various orders of Angels."[61]

According to Dionysius, these nine choirs are grouped into three hierarchies: The Supreme Hierarchy consisting of the Seraphim, Cherubim and Thrones; the Middle Hierarchy consisting of the Dominations, the Virtues, and the Powers, and; The Lower Hierarchy which is comprised of the Principalities, Archangels, and Angels.[62]

There is, however, some dispute as to whether this is a complete number of choirs with most believing that only God knows the exact number.

---

59 Ibid, pg. 35
60 Ibid, pg. 36
61 *The Angels*, pg. 49
62 Ibid, pg. 52

The Fall of Satan

Just like man, Angels were also required to prove their love for God during a period of testing. We are told that at the time of their test, "…they were not yet confirmed in grace and they did not enjoy the Beatific Vision during this time. This was a period of existence like that of our first parents before their fall…The Fathers and the theologians are unanimous in admitting a period of probation for the Angels" and that during this time, "some of the Angels sinned and were condemned to hell."[63]

The fact that the Angels sinned is proof that there was a time in their existence when sin was possible.

This is because the Beatific Vision is "the reward of the faithful whose loyalty to God has been tested during their early life…St. Thomas Aquinas was of the opinion that once in the possession of the Beatific Vision, a human soul or an angel can never be tempted to any evil whatsoever. In Heaven the Beatific Vision renders one completely, totally and perfectly satisfied and happy."[64] If the rebellious angels had beheld the Beatific Vision before the fall, they would never have been able to even aspire to being equal to, or greater than, God.

As a result of this rebellion, which was fueled by Satan's refusal to serve God, a great "war in heaven" broke out between the good angels and those who chose to follow Satan.

The Book of Revelation describes: "Then war broke out in heaven; Michael and his angels battled against the dragon. The dragon and its angels fought back, but they did not prevail and there was no longer any place for them in heaven. The huge dragon, the ancient serpent, who is called the Devil and Satan, who deceived the whole world was thrown down to earth, and its angels were thrown down with it."[65]

---

63 Ibid, pg. 45
64 Cruz, Joan Carroll, *Angels & Devils* (Charlotte, NC: Tan Books & Publishers, 1999) pg. 159
65 Revelation 12:7-9

However, this was not just some imaginary battle in the sky. As Dr. Kreeft describes: "Their war was a real war. It is not symbolic language. It was not a physical war, because angels do not have physical bodies, but it was a real war, a war of wills, of minds, like a war between paralyzed telepaths. The military symbols we use for it are not too strong but too weak...The war was more passionate, intense, and terrifying than any physical war or any physical symbol can convey."[66]

It is not known how many demons fell with Satan after that epic battle, only that there is a staggering number of Angels and a third of them fell.

Father Parente points out that "Only a number of the Angels fell, because only a number of them disobeyed and sinned; the others, the great majority of them, undismayed by the bad example given by some of their brethren, remained loyal to God, clinging to him with pure and ardent love."[67]

However, the number of those who did fall was indeed enormous. The late great exorcist of Rome, Father Gabriele Amorth, once wrote: "When someone asks me how many angels there are, I quote Revelation which speaks of myriads of myriads, an immense number, incomprehensible to our mind. When I am asked how many demons there are, I answer with the words that the demon himself spoke through a demoniac: 'We are so many that, if we were visible, we would darken the sun.'"[68]

For Satan, it was a long and dreadful fall. His name was Lucifer, or Light-bearer, and he was believed to have been the supreme Angel in the Choir of Cherubim.[69] He was "the greatest of all creatures, highest angel, Top Guy next to God – and *he* rebelled and invented evil."[70]

---

66 *Angels (and Demons)* pg. 118
67 *The Angels*, pg. 47
68 *An Exorcist: More Stories*, pg. 38
69 *The Angels*, pg. 57
70 Ibid, pg 118

His fateful fall, and that of the angels who chose to follow him, occurred as a result of a single choice "made with their whole mind and free will, which they could never take back because there was no ignorance, no temptation, no excuse, and no part of the self holding back."[71]

As the *Catechism of the Catholic Church* teaches, "It is the irrevocable character of their choice, and not a defect in the infinite divine mercy, that makes the angels' sin unforgiveable. 'There is no repentance for the angels after their fall, just as there is no repentance for men after death.'"[72]

From the moment of his fall, Satan has been the mortal enemy of God and man. He has devoted himself to destroying as much of God's kingdom as he can before Christ comes again in victory.

Adam Blai, Peritus of religious demonology and exorcism for the Roman Catholic Church, explains that these once-magnificent angels of God now "hate human beings with a complete and merciless passion. Their only goal for humans is to deceive and corrupt them into turning away from God so that they die in a poor spiritual state and become their eternal slave and victim."[73]

Demons go about this nefarious business by employing their angelic powers in what Pope St. Paul VI called a "predatory cunning" with which they "sow error, misfortune, decadence, and degradation in human history."[74]

Many people believe that because Satan fell, he and his legions were stripped of their angelic powers; however, this is not correct. As Father Delaporte writes, they did not lose all. "They lost their felicity; they did not lose all their power. Deprived

---

71 Ibid, pg. 116
72 *Catechism of the Catholic Church* (New York, NY: *Catholic Book Publishing Company*, 1994) No. 393
73 Blai, Adam C., M.S., *Possession, Exorcism, and Hauntings* (2014), pg. 82
74 *An Exorcist: More Stories*, pg. 68

of their personal gifts, they were not deprived of the faculties inherent in their nature."[75]

He uses the analogy of the once valiant soldier who failed in his duty and was stripped of his medals and uniform. Even though this soldier was dishonored and banished from the army, "he retains, nevertheless, his nature as man…So the demons, after their revolt had caused them to be expelled from heaven, remain such as they were originally constituted, that is to say, beings with an intelligence and a power superior to the intelligence and power of man."[76]

The retention of their preternatural capabilities is what makes Satan and his legions so enormously dangerous. These powers are what enable him to appear to man in a variety of clever disguises such as the person of Jesus Christ and the Blessed Virgin Mary, or even someone's deceased relative. These powers make him capable of funneling relevant information to psychics, mediums, and channelers, and can move the planchette on a Ouija board as readily as they can empower a curse or a spell.

It's important to know all this because when Satan and his followers fell, they did not fall into Hell. They fell to earth where they roam the world seeking souls who can be overcome and conquered by their super-human powers.

This explains why Jesus referred to Satan as "the ruler of this world"[77] and St. Paul called him the "god of this world"[78] rather than referring to him as the ruler or god of Hell.

"The book of Revelation is clear that after the war in heaven Lucifer and the errant angels were cast down to Earth to roam here and tempt mankind until the final judgment. It seems

---

[75] Delaporte, Rev. Father of the Society of Mary, *The Devil: Does He Exist and What Does He Do?* (Rockford, IL: *Tan Books and Publishers, Inc.*, 1982) pg. 21-22
[76] Ibid
[77] John 12:31
[78] 2 Cor 4:4

to be a common assumption or misunderstanding that demons are locked in hell; they are not."[79]

In his book, *Who is the Devil?* Nicholas Corte explains that "The kingdom of Satan is indeed Hell, but Satan received God's permission to recruit his subjects from the world."[80]

However, this doesn't mean that Satan is enjoying a "free ride." As Thomas Aquinas notes, "…[A[lthough the demons are not actually bound within the fire of hell while they are in this dark atmosphere, nevertheless their punishment is none the less; because they know that such confinement is their due. Hence, it is said in a gloss upon James 3:6: 'They carry fire of hell with them wherever they go."[81]

As we have just learned, Satan is well equipped for the task of recruiting subjects form the world and is particularly skilled in orchestrating the destruction he seeks to impart upon the world. This is why the fallen angels recognize him as their leader. Even though he led them to eternal damnation, the fallen angels are smart enough to realize that acting in chaos and division will not allow them to accomplish their ultimate mission to do maximum damage to God's Kingdom.

"… [I]t is believed that their fall did not impair their natural powers and that Lucifer still had the same power of influence among his brethren as he had before their fall – that his superior intelligence would make it clear to them that they could achieve more success and do more harm to souls by being organized and united, instead of being independent and divided. Lucifer, who was their superior in Heaven, was, and is now, their superior in Hell."[82]

In order to achieve maximum efficiency, St. Thomas Aquinas believed the devils also organized themselves into choirs

---

79 *Possession, Exorcism and Hauntings*, pg. 83
80 Corte, Nicholas, *Who is the Devil*, (Manchester, NH: *Sophia Institute Press*, 2013) pg. 58
81 Driscoll, Father Mike, *Demons, Deliverance and Discernment: Separating Fact from Fiction About the Spirit World* (El Cajon, CA: *Catholic Answers Press*, 2015) pg. 42
82 *Angels & Devils*, pg. 161

much like the Angels in Heaven, with some being more powerful than others. As the Saint wrote: "The demons are not equal in nature, and so among them there exists a natural precedence."[83]

Regardless of what rank they hold in their devilish choir, they put their immense preternatural powers to the most effective use.

"Satan can control the physical elements of earth. He has power to afflict with disease. He has the power to communicate with a human spirit – a power that Jesus illustrated in the parable of the sower: 'When anyone hears the word of the kingdom, and does not understand it, then the wicked one comes and snatches away what was sown in his heart ... (Matt 13:19)...Notice that Jesus does not say Satan steals the gospel out of the mind; he says Satan steals it *out of the heart*, or out of the spirit. Satan cannot read minds, but as a spiritual being, he can communicate to a human spirit. Jesus warned that Satan comes quickly after a Christian shares the gospel seed with an unbeliever and, if the unbeliever does not understand, Satan takes the words away through distractions, confusion, lies or substitutes for the truth."[84]

The evil one employs all of his formidable powers to trap the unwary human.

For example, while demons cannot foretell the future, they employ their intelligence with great cunning to predict the future simply by observation and deduction.[85] Demons are frighteningly astute at observing our personal habits, our tone of voice, facial expressions, and body language. They can overhear our conversations and everything we say when we're talking out loud to ourselves. They can read our text messages and journal entries. This information, combined with their superior intelligence and their acute perception of human behavior which they have been

---

83 Ibid, pg. 160
84 Martin, Walter; Rische, Jill Martin; Van Gorden, Kurt, *Kingdom of the Occult*, (Nashville, TN: *Thomas Nelson*, 2008) pg. 392
85 Fortea, Father Jose, *Interview with an Exorcist* (West Chester, PA: *Ascension Press*, 2006) pg. 17

observing since the dawn of creation, makes them capable of uncannily accurate predictions about what we will do.

"One might think of them as extremely accurate weathermen; they don't know the future, but they can make very good predictions."[86]

It also explains how, after being fed this information, psychics and mediums are sometimes able to make seemingly accurate predictions due to the intervention of demons.

One of Satan's greatest tricks is convincing people that he can heal. Only God can miraculously heal but Satan is an expert mimic and knows how to employ various sleights of hand to give the appearance of a genuine healing. For example, Scripture tells us that "Satan went out from the presence of the Lord and inflicted loathsome sores on Job from the sole of his foot to the crown of his head."[87] This tells us that sickness or injury can definitely originate from Satan if God allows it; therefore, it follows that Satan is capable of making a person feel better or even appear to be healed simply by stopping the sickness he is inflicting upon a person.

Because Satan is incapable of doing anything good, satanic "healings" are always accomplished by the power of suggestion, such as the placebo effect, or through an illusion of some kind. Even when he withdraws a sickness that he imposed, it is never to bring relief to the person but to trick them into believing in the use of illicit means such as magic or sorcery.

It's important to remember that Satan cannot work miracles because this is reserved to God; however, he has "…abilities not known to human beings, and these abilities may fool people into thinking they [demons] perform miracles. Demons can also trick our senses, making us think we are seeing and hearing things that aren't really there."[88]

---

86 *Demons, Deliverance, and Discernment*, pg. 42
87 Job 2:7
88 *Demons, Deliverance and Discernment*, pg. 43

This is because his preternatural powers make him a master of illusion. "For Satan himself transforms himself into an angel of light."[89] This mastery has spread much confusion among the faithful by tricking alleged psychics into believing they are receiving messages from God when they are actually being deceived by Satan. These messages are almost always couched in devout sounding language but contain theological errors that are often missed by the poorly catechized.

There are ample warnings about this aspect of Satan in Scripture. "For false christs and false prophets will rise and show great signs and wonders to deceive, if possible, even the elect,"[90] and "The coming of the lawless one is according to the working of Satan, with all power, signs, and lying wonders."[91]

The lawless one will mimic all the great miracles of Christ, such as walking on water, raising the dead, healing the sick, all of which will be lies worked via the preternatural powers of the angels of darkness that are so artful that even the elect will be fooled. Thankfully, our benevolent God has promised that He will shorten this time in order to spare the faithful. "And if those days had not been shortened, no one would be saved; but for the sake of the elect they will be shortened."[92]

Thankfully, Our Lord is a Good Shepherd who gives us ample warning about the characteristics of this mortal enemy of mankind to help us discern his wiles.

As He revealed in John's gospel: "He...does not stand in truth, because there is no truth in him. When he tells a lie, he speaks in character, because he is a liar, and the father of lies."[93]

This warning reminds us that since Satan is the enemy of good, "he is also the enemy of truth. What proceeds from his mouth are lies and half-truths. He tells no more truth than he

---

89 2 Cor 11:14
90 Matt 24:24
91 2 Thess 2:9
92 Math 24:22
93 John 8:44

needs to tell you in order to win you over," writes Catholic author John Labriola.[94]

Jesus also told us Satan "was a murderer from the beginning."[95]

This is because "his lies are designed to kill your soul, your spirit, your will, your mind, and your body. He wants to kill the life of grace in your soul, wipe it away. Though a murderer, he is not necessarily repulsive to the eyes and ears. He can speak quite smoothly and seductively and appear pleasing to the eyes. He's a patient assassin, a ruthless and relentless killer."[96]

The book of Revelation also describes Satan as "the accuser."

"For the accuser of our brothers has been cast down, he who accused them before our God day and night."[97]

"Satan's name means accuser. He accuses you before God, before yourself and before other men. He delights in disparaging your name, shaming your conscience and causing scandal in the Church," Labriola writes. "He accuses the innocent and the guilty, the humble and the proud. He knows your wounds and weaknesses. He'll exploit you with accusations of unworthiness and shame."[98]

Scripture also tells us he is a seducer who is always looking for ways to entice and deceive.

"And he was thrown out, that great dragon, that ancient serpent, who is called the devil and Satan, who seduces the whole world. And he was thrown down to the earth, and his angels were cast down with him."[99]

---

94 *Onward Catholic Soldier,* pg. 160
95 John 8:44
96 *Onward Catholic Soldier*, pg. 160
97 Rev 12:10
98 *Onward Catholic Soldier*, pg. 161
99 Rev. 12:9

Labriola writes: "Satan deceives at every opportunity without any shame; he is the great liar. He'll tell a partial truth to get you to believe a greater lie ... he is very skilled in the art of deception. His greatest deception is to convince you that he doesn't exist. This allows him to operate almost unimpeded."[100]

Almost is the operative word here. Satan and his legions can never have free reign over us. As powerful as they are, "demons are not chaotic random creatures that can afflict anyone at will; they are subservient creatures of God."[101] They are restricted by God and can only do what God allows.

But why would God allow demons to afflict us?

As Adam Blai explains: "God does not wish the demons to afflict humans, but his perfect justice allows it up to a point. He generally allows people to burn their hand on the stove when that is the only thing that will get through to them. He allows short term corrective pain because He will not violate our free will and force us to turn away from the demons. He hopes that when people experience the truth of a relationship with Satan they will come back to His loving arms."[102]

While we must respect the power of Satan, we must never give into a morbid fear of him because to do so would be to regard him as more powerful than the God Who created us and came to dwell within us by grace at the moment of our Baptism.

"...[F]or the one who is in you is greater than the one who is in the world."[103]

Satan is more aware of this than most Christians, which is why he fears the baptized Christian who is filled with the Spirit of God and relies upon Him for all that he will need in this world and the next.

---

100 *Onward Catholic Soldier*, pg. 164
101 *Possession, Exorcism, and Hauntings*, pg. 30
102 Ibid
103 1 John 4:4

Chapter Two

Ordinary Satanic Activity: Temptation to Acquire Hidden Powers

"He is the evil and cunning charmer who knows how to infiltrate everyone's individual psychology. He finds the open door and comes in: through our senses, our imagination, and our concupiscence."
– Pope St. Paul VI

The main tactic employed by Satan to impose his nefarious plans upon the world is through temptation. "A temptation is a thought, a feeling, an inclination, or a tendency that solicits us to violate the law of God for our own satisfaction."[104]

Temptation, known as "ordinary Satanic activity," is different from "extraordinary Satanic activity" (infestations, oppression, obsession, possession) which will be discussed in Chapter Four of this book.

While it might not sound as threatening as extraordinary Satanic activity, the ordinary activity of demons, which can come from the world and the flesh as well as the devil, has worked only too well throughout the history of man. Even the most fervent of souls such as Adam and Eve can be counted among those who fell for these so-called ordinary temptations. We all know the story of how God commanded them not to eat the fruit of the tree that

---
104 Michel, Father P.J., SJ, *Temptations: Where They Come From, What They Mean, and How to Defeat Them*, (Manchester, NH: *Sophia Institute Press*, 2016) pg. 5

stood in the middle of the garden because if they ate, or even touched its fruit, they would die.

The devil, hiding under the guise of a serpent, said to Eve, "You certainly will not die! God knows well that when you eat of it your eyes will be opened and you will be like gods, who know good and evil."[105]

He tempted Eve by appealing to her desire for knowledge and power and inspired within her just enough doubt about what God said to make her take the forbidden fruit.

"Behind the disobedient choice of our first parents lurks a seductive voice, opposed to God, which makes them fall into death out of envy."[106]

This same seductive voice has led to the downfall of many Christians, including the most devout. However, it's important to note that, even in the case of Adam and Eve, Satan was not solely to blame for the downfall of our First Parents. It was their own weaknesses that Satan exploited in order to make them fall victim to his schemes and so it is with the rest of us.

"Temptation properly so-called is rarely the exclusive work of the devil. Ordinarily he uses his knowledge of the dominant tendencies of a soul and his power over the senses in order to make an image more enticing, to stir up an impression, to intensify a pleasure, to quicken thus a desire, or make a solicitation more attractive and more actual, so that it will invade the field of conscience and gain the consent of the will."[107]

This explains why St. Paul never identifies sin with Satan. "In fact, he sees in sin first of all what it essentially is: a personal act of men, and also the state of guilt and blindness which Satan seeks effectively to cast them into and keep them in."[108]

---

105 Genesis 3:4
106 *Catechism*, No. 391
107 *I Want to See God,* pg. 106
108 *Christian Faith and Demonology*, pg. 13

The devil exercises only an influence over sinners, which is "…measured to the welcome which the individual gives to his inspiration. If people carry out his desires and do 'his work,' they do so freely."[109]

Regardless of how powerful it might be, temptation is only temptation. "Demons do not and cannot *cause* sin. Most theologians agree that they cannot directly influence our mind and will, but only our imagination, emotions, the material world around us, or in some cases, our bodies. They scare or deceive or tempt us into a choice, but this choice is ours."[110]

The devil can do nothing without our free will. "His force comes from our consent, and his weakness from our resistance."[111]

One of the reasons why temptation is so effective against the children of God is how craftily this monster of the dark goes about it.

"The devil is essentially a power of darkness. He works in the dark in order to surprise and trick. The success of his activities to win fervent souls depends on his cleverness in hiding what he is and what he is doing."[112]

We find in the temptation of Jesus an example of one person who didn't fall for it. This account of His temptation in the desert gives invaluable instruction to the faithful. It reads almost like a "how to" guide for discovering the wiles of Satan in order that we might be prepared. As Monsignor Leon Christiani writes in his book, *Evidence of Satan in the World*, Jesus was very deliberate about giving us this information.

---

109 Ibid, pg. 15
110 International Catholic Charismatic Renewal Services Doctrinal Commission, *Deliverance Ministry* (Vatican City: *ICCRS*, 2017) pg. 56
111 Christiani, Leon, *Evidence of Satan in the Modern World* (Rockford, IL: Tan Books and Publishers, Inc., 1961) pg. 12
112 P. Marie Eugene, OCD, *I Want to See God: A Practical Synthesis of Carmelite Spirituality, Volume 1* (Allen, TX: *Christian Classics*, 1953) pg. 104

"We should note...that there was no witness to this formidable encounter. The three Evangelists derived their account from Jesus himself. He took care to inform his disciples of what had passed between the Devil and himself. He wished them to know what he had seen, what it had meant to look each other... in the eye, to listen to Satan's attempts to subjugate him and make him deviate from his path. In a word, Christ had wished to be tempted. And he was. He revealed to his follows what this temptation had been."[113]

The famed exorcist, Father Jose Maria Fortea, explains that these three temptations symbolize the temptations the devout experience during the course of the spiritual life, although those endured by Jesus were especially subtle.

In the first temptation, the devil asks the Lord to change stones into bread and eat, thus breaking his fast. As Father Fortea points out, "the devil tempted Jesus not with sin *per se* but with imperfection. He was asked to stop doing a good, i.e., his fasting, and turn stones into bread."[114]

The devil also tempted Jesus by leading him up to a high place and showing him all the kingdoms of the earth. "All these things I shall give you if you will prostrate yourself and worship me," the devil promised.[115]

As Father Fortea explains, "Jesus was not asked to stop being God; he was only asked the sacrifice of humbling himself a little more. Could not the Just One who had made so many sacrifices for souls not do one more? It is the temptation to do a little evil so as to achieve a greater good."[116]

The devil then asked Jesus to throw himself down from a high parapet in order to prove to the world that he truly was the Son of God.

---

113 *Evidence of Satan in the World*, pg. 7-8
114 *Interview with an Exorcist*, pg. 62
115 Matt 4:8-9
116 *Interview with an Exorcist*, pg. 63

This temptation is one of pride and the desire to be publicly recognized.

"It was to prescind from the fact that it is God, in His time, who exalts His servants. Here the devil was saying, *Even though God decides the time and the moment, why not bring the moment forward? Why remain in obscurity when so much good can be done by coming out into the light in a glorious and spectacular way?* We can see that this third temptation is the most complex and subtle of all."[117]

These experiences of Jesus teach us about the subtleties of Satan and shine a bright light into the darkness that usually surrounds the machinations of evil. We must be constantly on our guard against this enemy who is not afraid to "think outside the box" when it comes to tempting the faithful. Satan and his minions use their mighty powers to tempt man in a variety of ways, some more subtle than others, however, they do have an overall game-plan, referred to by some as the "demonic doctrine" which consists of several non-negotiable points.

The primary doctrine of the demon is to *deny Jesus Christ*. Satan's aim is to convince people that Jesus is not the Son of the Most High and the Second Person of the Blessed Trinity. "This is the prime attack of Satan; he must undercut the person of the Master. He dares not allow the worship of the Lord Jesus, because he seeks worship for himself."[118]

The first part of the demonic doctrine follows this – assert that Jesus is *a* way, not *the* way. The New Age movement is spearheading this doctrine with its assertion that Jesus is just one of many prophets who is equal to Mohammed, the Buddha, Moses, and Mahatma Gandhi. The Mormons believe Jesus is one of many gods and Jehovah Witnesses say He's a super-angel named Michael.[119]

---

117 Ibid
118 Martin, Walter, Rische, Jill Martin, Van Gorden, Kurt, *Kingdom of the Occult* (Nashville, TN: *Thomas Nelson*, 2008) pg. 62
119 Ibid, pg. 59

A second part is to encourage the faithful to *pursue secret knowledge*. Book stores are filled with self-help books such as *The Secret* and *The Law of Attraction* that claim to have secret knowledge about how to use the power of the mind to achieve one's maximum potential and attract an abundance of wealth and good fortune. Known as the Human Potential Movement, it is one of the core components of the New Age movement and promotes a human-centered psychology based on the belief that a person is in complete control of their destiny. The devil is only too successful at convincing people that they "can obtain information from sources other than God and that this secret knowledge is reliable."[120] Evidence of their success can be found in the number of these books that have become bestsellers.

The third part is to encourage people to *explore powers other than God*. Satan is a big promoter of any divinatory practice that relies on powers that are not sourced in God: Ouija boards, tarot cards, psychics and channelers, etc. "One of the most successful demonic strategies is *absorption* – playing with something you cannot control. This absorption with occult power turns people away from the One who controls all things, in whose hands the Church must commit itself as witnesses and servants of Jesus Christ. The devil is engaged in trying to get people absorbed with the future, and the powers involved in revealing it."[121]

This part of the doctrine is particularly effective because of how attractive it is to the fallen nature of man and his propensity to obtain power. As the *Catechism* teaches, all forms of divination "conceal a desire for power over time, history, and in the last analysis, other human beings…"[122]

The fourth part is to *equate the Truth with mythology*. Just as St. Paul warned in Scripture, "…the time will come when people will not tolerate sound doctrine but, following their own

---

120 *Kingdom of the Occult*, pg. 59
121 Ibid, pg. 60
122 *Catechism of the Catholic Church* (New York, NY: *Catholic Book Publishing Company*, 1994), No. 2116

desires and insatiable curiosity, will accumulate teachers and will stop listening to the truth and will be diverted to myths."[123]

The Christian world is full of false teachers who are hawking their wares of deception in the form of books, *YouTube* videos, websites, and conferences, none of which conform to the authentic teaching of Jesus Christ. From false depictions of angels and preaching the "prosperity gospel" to incorporating non-Christian spiritualities derived from paganism or the East into the practice of Christianity, Satan has done a masterful job of diluting the faith and replacing the truth with trendy cultural movements that appeal to man's tendency to seek instant gratification and an escape from the Cross of Jesus Christ.

In essence, this doctrine can all be boiled down to three main principles that Satan has used to tempt man into sin from the beginning of time: "You can do all that you wish, no one has the right to command you, and you are the god of yourself."[124]

No one escapes the daily sundry temptations to sin such as encouraging people to gossip about their neighbors, steal from their employers, engage in promiscuous behavior, and take the Lord's name in vain. However, in today's secularized culture, where the concept of sin has become "hate speech" in some quarters, and the popular media is glamorizing a new "hipster occultism," the lure to pursue hidden powers and secret knowledge has become particularly attractive to our society, especially our youth.

Many are falling for Satan's "preferred method" throughout history which has always been to deceive and manipulate by enticing us "to become enchanters, Witches, soothsayers, omen interpreters, sorcerers, mediums, or Spiritists."[125]

This section will deal with the most serious of these temptations as they are manifesting today, beginning with the

---

123 2 Tim 4:3-4
124 Amorth, Fr. Gabrielewith Stefano Stimamiglio, *An Exorcist Explains the Demonic: The Antics of Satan and His Army of Fallen Angels* (Manchester, NH: *Sophia Institute Press*, 2016) pg. 30-31
125 *Kingdom of the Occult*, pg. 384

most dangerous, which is enticing the desperate to sell their soul to the devil in exchange for some believed good.

Contracts with the Devil

Evidence of people engaging in formal contracts with the devil has been around since as early as the fifth century AD. St. Jerome tells the story of a young man who went to a wizard to obtain the favor of a beautiful woman and who willingly paid for these services by renouncing his faith in Jesus Christ. Then there was the pitiful story of St. Theophilus (d. 538), a parish priest who sold his soul to the devil in exchange for the return of his position in the Church, a deal he eventually retracted. Sister Magdalena of the Cross (1487-1560) made a pact with the devil at the age of twelve and fooled some of the greatest clerical and secular minds of her time with her miracles and prophecies until finally confessing to her sin.

Unfortunately, pacts with the devil are not confined to the Middle Ages but continue to this day. As mentioned in the introduction to this study, a popular video game entitled *Techno's Deception: Invitation to Darkness*, actually requires players to "make an unholy pact and sell their soul to Satan in exchange for power" with the object of the game being to ensure the resurrection of Satan and obtain his power.[126] It seems hard to believe that such a game even exists, let alone that it is rated "T" for teen.

There is no denying the fact that there are people who, with full awareness and consent, make a pact with the devil and devote their souls to him in order to achieve something in return, whether that be power, money, a love interest, or some other special favor.

According to St. Thomas Aquinas, these pacts are distinguished between *express* contracts and those that are *implied* or *understood*.

---

[126] Nunneley, Stephany, "Videogames are being used by Satan to steal your soul," *VG24/7*, February 27, 2010

"When the devil appears under a visible form, converses with the unfortunate being who has called upon him discusses with him the conditions of his unhallowed favors, and receives in return a promise of obedience, an abjuration of baptism, there is an express contract. The contract is implicit when, with the legitimate suspicion that Satan is playing a part in certain mysterious practices such as diverse modes of incantation by the wand, by cards, by table-turning, recourse is still had to those practices."[127]

Those who enter into pacts with the devil may appear to get what they want, but their wishes are granted at an eternal cost to themselves. Although many are duped into thinking the devil can grant them whatever they desire, this is not true. His goal is only to destroy.

"...[T]he power of the devil is limited. Worldly success depends on a complex interplay of causes and effects. The devil can only tempt humans to be part of his plan..."[128]

He may tempt a woman to fall for a man who is desiring her, but he can't force her to do this. Nor can he convince a boss to give one man a promotion over another. He can only tempt, but he cannot coerce. This means that the person who sold his soul to the devil for a favor may find out, when it's too late, that the devil is unable to deliver what was promised.

As Father Fortea reveals, "Making a pact with the devil does not mean that you will obtain a life of wealth, luxury, or fame. I personally know of two people who made such a pact, and to put it frankly, their material lifestyle is worse than mine...We need to remember that the devil is a deceiver; he is not God – he cannot give whatever he wants (See Catechism No. 395)."[129]

Father Fortea believes the greatest destructive power of the demonic pact is that the person may think they are condemned and beyond forgiveness. This is not true!

---
127 The Devil, pg. 61-62
128 *Interview with an Exorcist*, pg. 30
129 Ibid, pg. 29

"A person can always repent of the pact whenever he wants to with a simple act of the will. Upon repenting, the pact they made remains as ink on paper, no matter what the terms of the deal were. Even if the possibility of repentance was excluded in the pact, such a clause is useless. God has given us the freedom to do as we want; we cannot renounce this gift…"[130]

Although making a pact with the devil is not their exclusive purview, this is a practice most commonly employed by Satanists.

Satanism

Satanism refers to people, groups or movements, whether isolated or in organized groups, who practice some form of veneration or evocation of the devil regardless of whether or not they believe he is a personal being.

"Such an entity is generally understood by the Satanists as a being or metaphysical force, or a mysterious innate element of a human being, or an unknown natural energy that is evoked by diverse proper names (e.g., Lucifer) through the use of certain ritual practices."[131]

The cult of Satan, or Satan worship, is in part a survival of the ancient worship of demons and in part a revolt against Christianity. The history of early Satanism is obscure. It arose about the 12th century in Europe and was revived in the reign of Louis XIV in France and is still practiced by various groups throughout the world.[132]

There are essentially two different kinds of Satanism – *theistic* and *religious*.

Theistic Satanism, which is the least common of the two, concerns those people who actually worship the devil. One of the best examples of this type of Satanism is the *Temple of Set*.

---

130 Ibid
131 Ibid
132 "Satanism," *Columbia Encyclopedia*

This satanic church was founded in the United States by Michael Aquino after a falling out with Howard Stanton LaVey, also known as Anton Szandor LaVey, the founder of *The Church of Satan*. Aquino was dissatisfied with LaVey's version of Satanism because he felt it was more like a business venture than a religion. However, because he knew that any attempt to start up another Church of Satan would be futile, Aquino decided to summon up the Prince of Darkness and ask him what to do.

"On the eve of the north solstice, June 21, 1975, Aquino performed a magical Working and Satan purportedly appeared to him in the image of Set – the oryx-headed god of death and destruction that Aquino claims is the earliest manifestation of the Christian devil," writes Richard G. Howe of the *Christian Research Institute*.[133]

During this appearance, which is recounted in Aquino's book entitled *The Book of Coming Forth by Night*, Set told him to leave LaVey and start the age of Set. Although much more secretive than religious Satanism, it has even begun to distance itself from the term Satanism, but their philosophy is definitely of the "left-hand path" meaning it worships the self and glorifies the temporal rather than the spiritual. It is a complex system of philosophies through which one seeks to realize one's own divinity and readily seeks the counsel of the Prince of Darkness.[134]

Religious Satanism is comprised of those people who accept Satan as a pre-Christian life-principal who is worth emulating. Although theistic Satanists follow a number of religious traditions, the largest by far is *The Church of Satan* which was founded by Anton LaVey.

LaVey and his followers do not believe in the existence of Satan which is why they do not worship the devil. In his *Satanic Bible*, LaVey lays out his views, "…which can best be described

---

133 Howe, Richard G., "Satanism: A Taste for the Dark Side," *Christian Research Institute*, Article JAS006
134 Ibid

as an atheistic religion of self-interested hedonism with a dash of occult philosophy," writes Howe.

LaVey's book, which has been in continuous print since it first appeared in 1970 and has been translated into a number of other languages, contains nine basic statements[135] that form the basis of LaVey's philosophy:

1. Satan represents indulgence instead of abstinence.

2. Satan represents vital existence instead of spiritual pipe dreams.

3. Satan represents undefiled wisdom instead of hypocritical self-deceit.

4. Satan represents kindness to those who deserve it instead of love wasted on ingrates.

5. Satan represents vengeance instead of turning the other cheek.

6. Satan represents responsibility to the responsible instead of concern for psychic vampires.

7. Satan represents man as just another animal, sometimes better, more often worse than those that walk on all fours, because of his "divine spiritual and intellectual development," has become the most vicious animal of all.

8. Satan represents all of the so-called sins, as they all lead to physical, mental or emotional gratification.

9. Satan has been the best friend the Church has ever had, as he has kept it in business all these years.[136]

People who practice Satanism do not necessarily fall neatly into one of these two categories. Instead, they splinter off into their own groups, with their own philosophies, such as the New York-based Satanic Temple which practices a kind of

---

135 *Kingdom of the Occult*, pg. 415
136 Ibid

political satanism. This group is famous for staging black masses and challenging public displays of the 10 Commandments with a bronze sculpture depicting Baphomet, the goat-headed symbol of Satan. It also challenges Christian after-school groups in public schools with After School Satan clubs.

Experts say that the people who are most attracted to Satanism tend to be teens and young adults who are from white, middle to upper-middle class families, and who are bright and do well in school.[137]

Initiation into Satanism usually requires the committing of a crime such as setting fire to a dumpster or spray painting symbols on a church. From this point, the newcomer will learn satanic prayers, and how to conjure spells, curses and incantations that promise everything from success to the destruction of enemies. Most of these practices are found in LaVey's *Satanic Bible* or *The Satanic Ritual*, both of which are heavily relied upon in the realms of Satan worship. It is through these various forms of ritual magic that Satan uses manifestations of his power to beguile the unwary.

"The most intriguing rituals for youth seem to be the animal sacrifice, the spilling of blood, drinking of blood, and eventually the eating of animal parts, all to gain supernatural power. They will be taught that the life forces are contained in the blood, and that these forces can be taken into their bodies by consuming blood or eating specific body organs, such as the heart. Writings also explain that energy will be released into the air by torturing. Screams and cries release energy that can be absorbed into their own bodies and they can become stronger and more powerful. The convert will be instructed that his new god demands sacrifices for the rituals to work."[138]

Practitioners of Satanism normally construct an altar where they conduct a variety of rituals. Special clothing must be worn such as black robes or other dark attire which

---

[137] Wise, Russ, "Satanism: The World of the Occult", *Probe Ministries*, available on the website at www.probe.org
[138] Ibid p. 215

symbolizes the power of darkness. Black and white candles are used, but no more than one white candle can be lit during a ritual. The black candle represents the light and wisdom of Satan and the white candle represents the followers of Christ and is used for their destruction.[139]

The chalice or cup is another item needed and all types are acceptable except gold, because gold represents Heaven. Anything can be drunk from the cup as long as it intensifies one's feelings, such as alcohol or other drugs. The last item on the list is a sword or knife, which symbolizes force.

The black mass is considered to be the principal rite of every satanic group. The rite is usually officiated by a celebrant, a deacon and a subdeacon who is usually a Satanist and can also be a person who is possessed by the devil.[140] The instruments used include candles, an inverted pentacle, a chalice full of wine or liquor, a bell, a sword, an aspergillum (used to sprinkle water) and an inverted crucifix. An authentically consecrated Host is also used. The altar is a nude woman and all participants wear black clothes with a hood.

"The rite follows more or less that of the Catholic Mass with the prayers recited in Latin, English and French. Instead of the name of God the name of Satan is invoked, together with the names of various demons, the Our Father is pronounced in the contrary or negative sense (our father who art in hell), invectives are hurled against Jesus Christ and the Host is profaned in various ways (utilizing it in sexual practices, trampling it repeatedly with hate)."[141]

These rituals also parody the Church in that they are tied to particular feast days. The most important one is on the Eve of All Saints, also known as Halloween, which is considered the "magic New Year." The night before February 2nd, which is the feast of the Presentation of Jesus in the Temple, is known as the "magic

---

139 Ibid, p. 214
140 *An Exorcist Explains the Demonic*, pg. 37
141 Ferrari, Giuseppe "Phenomenon of Satanism in Contemporary Society"

spring"; and the "summer magic" occurs on the night between April 30 and May 1. Satanists also conduct rituals on nights when the new moon is inaugurated because it is particularly dark.[142]

Once one becomes involved in Satanism, it is particularly difficult to leave the practice, not only because most groups threaten members with death but because of the catastrophic harm done to the soul. A variety of afflictions manifest in people who worship Satan ranging from depression and suicidal tendencies to outright possession.

"Consecration to Satan, a pact of blood with him, and participation in satanic rites or attending satanic schools ... to become priests of Satan are all direct and willful ties," writes Father Amorth. "Healing requires decisive rejection of Satan, renewal of baptismal promises, and reparation of all evil committed against God and neighbor."[143] This reparation must include sacramental Confession.

Cases of diabolical infestation or possession may require special intervention by priests trained in the rite of exorcism.

Because the devil knows that the plunge into outright Satanism may be too much for many, he tempts them with the various means his followers use to exert power over others. By far, the most popular today, is the practice of sorcery.

Sorcery

Although today's popular occult-fiction books such as the Harry Potter series make wizardry look like child's play, engaging in any type of sorcery is fraught with danger which is why it is expressly forbidden by the Church.

"All practices of magic or sorcery, by which one attempts to tame occult powers, so as to place them at one's service and have a supernatural power over others – even if this were for the

---
142 *An Exorcist Explains the Demonic,* pg. 37
143 *An Exorcist: More Stories,* p. 113

sake of restoring their health – are gravely contrary to the virtue of religion. These practices are even more to be condemned when accompanied by the intention of harming someone, or when they have recourse to the intervention of demons."[144]

The reason for this strict condemnation is based on "… revelation and the conviction that in spiritism and occultism it is the devil who is acting."[145]

Not to be confused with stage magic, which is based in illusion rather than the occult, the type of magic known as sorcery is designed to exert power over another – whether that be for something good or evil. Although some like to differentiate magic according to its uses, such as to call it "white" or "black" magic, in reality, there is no such distinction.

Father Fortea explains: "In popular language, *white magic* is said to be magic that is used for good whereas black *magic* is used for evil. But both types of "magic" are useless. Strictly speaking, any paranormal effect achieved through magic is accomplished through the intervention of demons, not as a result of a particular person's "magical" powers. Even if those who practice magic - witches, sorcerers, seers, etc. – deny it (or are even unaware of it), the devil is behind all their works. And the very magic they practice in the end opens them up to demonic influence and even possession."

Typical, magic is worked through the utilization of spells, curses, charms, invocations and rituals, crystal balls, etc. These various methods are used to modify the course of human events by resorting to preternatural powers. Because the good angels exist solely to do the Will of God, and God explicitly forbids the use of sorcery in Deuteronomy 18:10, the only other source of preternatural power is the devil, which is why Satan is believed to be the force behind the machinations of sorcery.

---

144 *Catechism of the Catholic Church*, No. 2117
145 *An Exorcist Explains the Demonic*, pg. 38

A person learns how to practice the art of wizardry through a type of "bona fide initiation, along with courses that introduce a person to this 'art.'"[146]

There are two different kinds of magic: *imitative* and *contagious*.

Imitative magic is based on the concept of similarity in form and practice. It rests on the principle that everything generates something similar. An example of this are puppets used as a symbol for a person which is then pierced with pins in order to hurt or kill them.

Contagious magic is based on the principle of physical contact or contagion. This form requires the use of objects belonging to the target, such as nail clippings, hair, a photograph. "...[T]he sorcerer will use the appropriate rituals or formulas during pre-established times of the year and day. The evil work will come to fruition through the intervention of the spirits that he invokes."[147]

The exercising of these notorious talents is what gains the sorcerer his prominence. "He is expected to exercise a certain control over illness, natural forces, and even over meteorology."[148]

While he may indeed be powerful, thanks to the intervention of Satan, there is one thing that the wizard cannot do – he cannot reverse the working of his magic.

"...[A]ll the consequences of the occult – possessions, obsessions, the evil eye, strange powers, and similar things – having been caused by the influence of Satan and activated by wizards, cannot, evidently, be reversed by them. On the contrary, their interventions would only worsen things."

This is because the person working the magic does not have mastery over the spirits that are being invoked.

---

146 *An Exorcist Explains the Demonic*, pg. 46-47
147 *An Exorcist Tells His Story*, pg. 144-145
148 *Evidence of Satan in the World*, pg. 65

"We must not imagine that people invoking evil spirits over others actually have mastery over these spirits. In fact, it is the reverse: whoever has recourse to evil spirits by pronouncing a curse or casting a spell is progressively taken control of by those spirits."[149]

The most common way that a sorcerer uses his power is in the working of spells.

Spells

A magic spell is a generic reference which includes all forms of magic which a sorcerer might use to bring either evil or "good" upon a person. These include the evil eye, curses, "love potions," and the like.

The working of a spell tends to mimic Catholic sacraments which is why it has similar requirements which must be fulfilled before it can become potent.

First, just as sacraments have visible signs, such as the bread and wine used in the Eucharist, spells have theirs, such as clothing, photos, personal items, and food. These items are then cursed or prayed over by the wizard, much like the priest prays over the bread and wine; only in this case, the sorcerer relies on his faith in the power of the devil rather than in God.

"...[T]he wizard must 'win over' the action of the evil spirit, pressing it into service with invocations and prayers."[150]

Similarly, just as a priest uses a sacramentary which contains the text of the various rites, the wizard relies on the grimoire which is a book containing the text and required rituals of a variety of spells. There are dozens of grimoires such as *The Egyptian Secrets of Albertus Magnus*, *The Black Books of Elverum*, and *The Arbatel of Magic*.[151]

---

149 *Deliverance Ministry*, pg. 71
150 *An Exorcist Explains the Demonic*, pg. 41
151 *The Grimoire Encyclopedia*, accessed online.

In addition to recorded spells, sorcerers can create their own spells with the main requirement being the need to have a firm intention.

"Spell-casting is the art of identifying, raising, and directing energy to actualize our intentions ... Your magickal intention is the foundation of any spell."[152]

After establishing the intention, the spellcaster must then decide what materials are needed, such as candles, crystals, etc. Also to be determined is the timing of the spell, whether it should be cast during a particular time of day, moon phase, etc. The wording of the spell is also important because it indicates what powers are to be called upon when working the spell.

Curses come in a wide variety and are imposed through spells or other means.

As Father Gabriele Amorth explains in his book, *An Exorcist Tells His Story*, some curses are referred to as "illness" because they are used to make someone sick. Another type of curse is called "divisive" because it's meant to divide people such as spouses or families. Death curses are called "destruction" because they destroy the recipient. There are four main categories of curses, some of which can be conjured independent of a sorcerer.

1. Curses imposed through the use of black magic, witchcraft or satanic rites that culminate with black masses are considered to be the most powerful. "Their common characteristic is to obtain a curse against a specific person through magic formulas or rituals – at times very complex – by invoking the demon ..." explains Father Amorth.[153]

2. Curses that are spoken between people who have a blood relationship with one another are particularly damaging. For instance, in one case, a father who did not want a child wished

---

152 Faragher, Aliza Kelly, "A Modern Witch's Guide to Casting Love Spells," *Allure*, May 21, 2018
153 Amorth, Father Gabriele, *An Exorcist Tells His Story* (San Francisco, CA: *Ignatius Press*, 1999) pg 129-130

evil upon his newborn son and continued to do so as long as the boy lived at home. As he grew up, the boy suffered every kind of ill fortune in life – poor health, chronic unemployment, a difficult marriage, sickly children. Father Amorth said the exorcism helped him spiritually, but nothing more, and that his life remained a train wreck.

3. The hex (also known as malefice) is another means and is the most common way that a curse is imposed. The name malefice is Latin for *male factus* which means to do evil, and involves creating an object out of certain materials such as burned powders, animal bones, herbs, etc. that symbolize the will to harm. These are offered to Satan to be imprinted with his powers.

This spell can be cast *directly*, such as by mixing the object used for the spell into the victim's food or drink. People who are afflicted with a curse in this way often have a characteristic stomach ache with which exorcists are very familiar. A spell can be imposed *indirectly* by hexing objects that belong to the target such as photographs, clothes, or dolls that represent the person. In the latter case, pins are thrust into the doll in various locations causing victims to suffer from intense headaches, stomach aches, etc.

4. The evil eye is a spell cast just by looking at someone with evil intention. "The evil eye is a true spell," Father Amorth writes. "In other words, it presupposes the will to harm a predetermined person with the intervention of demons."[154] Belief in the evil eye is as much cultural as it is spiritual and variations of it can be found among the Portuguese, Turks, Egyptians, Scandinavians, and especially the Middle East from where it is believed to originate. Devices said to protect against the evil eye have become a cottage industry with talismans of all shapes and sizes being sold around the world. Because these objects are used in superstitious ways, their use only compounds the problem.

The best defense against the curse, regardless of where it originates, is to remain close to God in prayer. "...[C]urses are effective only if God allows them to have effect," writes Father

---

154 *An Exorcist Tells His Story*, pg. 132

Fortea. "The more one prays, the more one will be protected against these things."[155]

Witchcraft/Wicca

Sometimes referred to as the Goddess movement or Goddess spirituality, many of today's witches belong to a modern subset of witchcraft known as Wicca. Wicca is derived from the old English word "wic a" meaning "witch," and is a form of modern religious witchcraft that was originally meant to be a goddess-centered nature religion. It has since become just one of a wide collection of ancient beliefs and occult practices that fall under the umbrella of "neo-paganism."

Particularly popular today among teen girls and young women, the devil has made modern witchcraft into an almost irresistible temptation to young women who are seeking empowerment in the age of #MeToo. Numerous young enthusiasts, referred to as "hipster witches," have been recruited and engage in everything from sorcery and herbalism to channeling and massage. Elements of ancient Celtic, Greek, Roman and Egyptian religions can be found in the toolbox of today's witch along with traditions such as Shamanic Healing Circles and Toltec Wisdom.[156]

Like the neo-pagan movement to which it belongs, the hallmark of modern witchcraft is diversity.

"Witchcraft is individualistic to the point of being anarchic," writes author Alexander Brooks, "with no centralized authority or even any agreed-upon definition of what a 'Witch' is. In effect, a witch is whoever says they are a witch, and witch beliefs and practices amount to whatever individual witches actually believe and do."[157]

---

155 *Interview with an Exorcist,* pg. 110
156 Alexander, Brooks, *Witchcraft Goes Mainstream* (Eugene, OR: *Harvest House Publishers*, 2004) p. 33
157 Ibid, p. 35

The witches of today may be as eclectic as the Craft itself, but there remain four basic tenets that can be ascribed to the neo-pagan belief system of modern witchcraft.

First is a belief that divinity is inherent in all of nature (called animism/polytheism/pantheism); second, it is female-centered and goddess oriented; third, it does not believe in the concept of sin and the uniqueness of Christ; and fourth it believes in spiritual reciprocity or "what goes around comes around."

There is no central authority or established organization in the Wiccan religion and the internet is its unofficial "church." A random Google search lists nearly 200,000 sites for witchcraft and slightly more for Wicca. There are sites for people of all ages, complete with chat rooms, coven-finders, and bulletin boards.

Although not all witches belong to covens, those who do tend to form groups of about 13 people.

"The covens are governed by a high priestess and a high priest, with the high priestess being the leading figure in the coven," writes Donald H. Thompson, retired police officer and cult expert for the Baltimore police department. "Their purpose is to guide members to achieve a nature-based attitude and to instruct them in the ways of the Craft, with its rituals and initiations."[158]

These rituals are numerous, Thompson writes. "There are rituals for initiation, rituals for healing and protection, rituals for the sun and the sea, and it goes on and on. You can look at witchcraft as a religion expressed in rituals."

Rituals are commonly held in homes or out in the open with some being conducted "skyclad" (naked).

"Witchcraft rituals and spells are often (but not always) performed within a circle referred to as *compass round* or *circle round*; they can be 'cast' individually or by a high priestess who is usually the chief authority figure within a coven. Innumerable

---

158 Gesy, Father Lawrence J. *Today's Destructive Cults and Movements*, p. 206

belief systems exist within the millions of sects currently under the umbrella of Neopaganism, but the heart of their teachings is essentially goddess/god worship. They supplant the authority of the God of the Bible with the authority of goddesses and – to a lesser extent – gods, drawing from a long history of pagan cultures, rituals, and folklore. But no matter what label they may claim, the Bible teaches they are essentially mediums invoking a power other than the power of God; sorcerers, in the classic sense of the biblical term."[159]

Witches also engage in practices designed to increase their powers of clairvoyance and divination.

The quest for power has tempted whole cultures into forming an alliance with occult powers, such as the worldwide prevalence of practices such as voodoo, Santeria, and traditional religions rooted in shamanism.

Vodun (Voodoo)

This form of sorcery is mainly associated with the island nation of Haiti even though it has spread to many other countries in the last 200 years. More than just a spiritual practice, it is a way of life for the Haitian people who resort to it to maintain health and personal well-being.

"'To achieve this end, Vodunists establish and maintain contact with cosmic entities they call *lwa*.' The *lwas* or *loas* are disembodied spirits, deities that may be classified as either good or bad in practice but in Vodun basic theology, remain essentially neutral. *Lwas* also act as intermediary spirits that can communicate to the Vodunist, an occult experience that reinforces the reality of the existence of *lwa* and the validity of Vodun."[160]

It is the West Indies branch of vodun that saw the intermingling of voodoo with Catholicism. It occurred when

---

159 *The Kingdom of the Occult*, pg. 443
160 *The Kingdom of the Occult*, pg. 490

African slaves arrived in Haiti in the 18th century to work the sugar can fields and were baptized into the Catholic Church. However, plantation owners could not communicate Catholicism in its fullness, "so the slaves received only fragments of doctrinal truth"[161] which they adapted to fit the Catholic mold, thus becoming what is known as Caribbean Vodun.

"The full expression of Vodun worship comes through dance, song, and ritual drums, all of which have been routinely misinterpreted by outsiders. The dance forms a connection and communication between the participant and the spirit world, especially during rituals and ceremonies. Vodun theology contains hundreds of spirit-gods, too numerous to list, some of which represent nature…animals…and departed humans."[162]

Santeria is a form of voodoo which blends Yoruba and Catholic beliefs. It is primarily associated with people living in Cuba and the West Indies and emphasizes the occult, demonic possession and trance states which are used to communicate with the deceased.

"Santeria worship involves drumming and dancing as essential rituals. By dancing the practitioner expresses the *ashe* [energy] of the universe and calls into presence the power of the Orisha (gods)…The highest god, *Oludmare,* is not directly worshiped, but is invoked in various rituals. The *Orisha* (thousands of gods) are directly worshiped and they progressively increase in power through worship. *Orisha* guides or leads the participant to fulfill their destiny."[163]

Shamanism

Shamanism is based on animism, a belief that all created things have a soul and consciousness. Mountains, woods, forests,

---

161 Ibid, 491
162 Ibid, 492
163 *The Kingdom of the Occult*, pg. 489

rivers, and lakes are perceived to possess spirits and to be living, thinking impassioned beings like man.[164] Animists believe the world is pervaded by these spiritual forces that hover about man at all times and are the cause of his mishaps, pains and losses.

Because man is thought to be helpless against these spirits, he relies on the services of a shaman who knows the appropriate words and acts to perform that shield man from harm and envelope him in a kind of protective armor so that the evil spirits become inactive or at least inoffensive.[165]

The shaman is known by a variety of names – holy man, priest, medicine man, even the pejorative "witch doctor." It is the shaman's responsibility to find the most beautiful, loving, healing, wise and powerful spirits to help man contend with a variety of ills.

"A shaman knows his spirits intimately by name," writes Mark Andrew Ritchie in the *Christian Research Journal*. "He speaks to them daily and even views them as his alter ego. Hallucinogenic drugs are often part of the ritual in which he interacts with his spirits for guidance. Whenever he has a problem his spirits cannot solve, they summon another spirit that can solve it."[166]

The shaman is a healer, an educator, a keeper of the myths, traditions and tribal wisdom of his people and a master in the art of divination. He is believed to possess secret knowledge and to have the power of assuming other shapes and of employing souls of the dead.[167]

There are several means by which a shaman controls the spirits. The most common is symbolic magic which is based on the principle that association in thought must involve a similar connection in reality. For instance, placing "magical" fruit-shaped stones in a garden is thought to insure a good crop. To bring about

---

164 "Shamanism," the *Catholic Encyclopedia*
165 Ibid
166 Ritchie, Mark Andrew, "Shamanism: Eden or Evil?" *Christian Research Journal*, Vol. 25: No. 4, 2003
167 "Shamanism," *The Catholic Encyclopedia*

someone's death, symbolic magic calls for the creation of a doll-like image of the person, then piercing it with sharp instruments.[168]

Fasting with solitude is another method. This is usually accompanied by bodily cleanness and incantations in some ancient language. Among the Indo-Europeans, these incantations are known as mantras. Sometimes the shaman will mimic the sounds of the object of nature where the spirits are thought to reside, e.g., the whispering wind, a growling bear, a screeching owl.[169]

Dances and contortions with rattles and drums are also common. The Ojibwa Indians all rise at the sound of the sacred drum which alerts them to the presence of the Great Spirit. The frenzied pace of these dances is meant to invoke an ecstatic state. Some tribes, such as those in South America, use drugs to induce this state.[170]

Possession by a spirit is another device. In some cultures, such as Korea, the shaman is thought to have power over the spirits only because he or she is possessed by a more powerful demon.[171]

Not all men can be tempted to satiate their thirst for power by becoming directly involved with Satan as in the examples cited above. The evil one knows that some men are more easily tempted to gain influence over others through what they believe to be less dangerous ways, such as through the acquisition of special knowledge.

---

168 Ibid
169 Ibid
170 Ibid
171 Ibid

Chapter Three

Ordinary Satanic Activity:
Temptation to Acquire Secret Knowledge

"Today we would rather appear strong, daring. We pose as positive, concrete individuals while, at the same time, putting our faith in all sorts of gratuitous magical and popular whims, in superstition such as: beware of the number thirteen; beware of this or that! We believe in imaginary entities, to which we pay exaggerated, almost ridiculously scrupulous observance. On the other hand, when the Lord says: 'Watch out, there is much more than this!' we refuse to believe. Why?"

– Pope St. Paul VI

The quest for secret knowledge has always been a temptation for man and has caused him to turn to a wide variety of tools with which to acquire it. Whether it's the temptation to garner knowledge or to uncover the secrets of the Universe, Satan is a master at tempting the faithful to put their trust in anyone or anything other than God. He offers them a wide array of psychics and astrologers, Ouija boards, New Age self-help books, Eastern meditation techniques, anything that promises enlightenment about oneself, the human mind, and the Universe.

Satan's preferred means to tempt people to seek special knowledge is through the practice of divination which is "any means of predicting an unknown event with the aid of physical objects or events that are read or interpreted, such as tarot cards, runes, crystal gazing, omens, scrying, palmistry, and dreams."[172]

Divination is especially dangerous because "...once a person begins to divine, a spiritual door or portal opens between the material world and the spiritual world," explains Father Algaier. "Without divination, demons must content themselves to work in the world indirectly, mostly by enticing humans to sin. The more humans sin, the more evil is brought into the world... But even in a world thoroughly obsessed with sin, demons still must work indirectly. That all changes when the portal between the material world and the spiritual world is opened. The most common way this happens is through divination. Once that door is opened and a demon 'gets a foot inside,' resealing that portal can be remarkably difficult. In addition, the more a person divines, the more times the door is opened. This increases opportunities for demons to work directly and can also increase the frequency and intensity of a demon's activity."[173]

It's important to remember that because the future is known only to God, all efforts to know the future are considered to be divination.

As the *Catechism* teaches, "Any attempt...that man makes to know the future on his own, other than what we know from Scripture and predictions of the Saints, involves *superstition* (belief in meaningless indications), *idolatry* (placing false trust in people or techniques instead of in God, and *demonology* (commerce with evil spirits). All of these are forbidden by the First Commandment of God and are therefore under the condemnation of the Catholic Church."[174]

For this reason, "All forms of divination are to be rejected: recourse to Satan or demons, conjuring up the dead or other practices falsely supposed to "unveil" the future. Consulting

---

[172] *Kingdom of the Occult*, pg. 196
[173] Algaier, Father Robert, "The Ouija Board: A Game or a Gamble?" *Envoy Magazine*, May/June, 2000
[174] *Angels and Devils*, pg. 279

horoscopes, astrology, palm reading, interpretation of omens and lots, the phenomena of clairvoyance, and recourse to mediums all conceal a desire for power over time, history, and, in the last analysis, other human beings, as well as a wish to conciliate hidden powers. They contradict the honor, respect, and loving fear that we owe to God alone." [175]

This chapter will focus on the most prevalent forms of divination in practice today.

Astrology

Astrology is the single most popular form of divination, even among Christians. An ancient Babylonian occult art, it is believed to have originated with the pagan Chaldeans who observed the orderly movement of the planets, assigned them godlike characteristics and powers, and eventually began to worship them as gods. Astrologers would then interpret the pattern of the planets as omens or signs of what was to come.[176]

Astrologers believe that the location of planets in relation to the constellations of the zodiac have a particular influence on each person at the moment of their birth. By studying the stars and planets associated with a person's birth date, they believe they can predict the events likely to occur in a person's life based upon the movement of the stars and planets.

The two most popular branches of predictive astrology are known as *natal astrology* and *mundane astrology*.

"*Natal astrology*...makes a prediction based on a person's character, present situation or future outlook beginning with a birth date...*Mundane astrology* usually makes a prediction on a larger scale for a national, civil, or political leadership future."[177]

---

175 *Catechism of the Catholic Church*, No. 2116
176 Montenegro, Marcia, "Astrology: What it Really Is," published on the *CANA* website at www.christiananswersforthenewage.org/Articles_Astrology.html
177 *Kingdom of the Occult*, pg. 271

The horoscope is by far the most popular form of astrological prediction. A person can visit an astrologer and have a natal or birth chart made for them which is an individual character analysis and prediction about the future.

General horoscopes can be found in newspapers, magazines and on the Internet which contain predictions based on the twelve zodiac signs: Aries, Cancer, Taurus, Leo, Pisces, Gemini, Virgo, Libra, Capricorn, Aquarius, Scorpio, and Sagittarius.

The problem with these zodiac signs is that they are based on flawed science. As Father Mitch Pacwa points out in his book, *Catholics and the New Age*, the actual zodiac is an imaginary circle around the ecliptic of the earth's annual trip around the sun. Astrologers artificially divided it into 12 equal sections of 30 degrees each even though astronomers know this is not the case. The actual degrees of the constellations range anywhere from 7.0 to 37.5.

According to astronomers, because the actual belt (ecliptic) of the zodiac has altered its former relationship to the earth by about 36 degrees west, "Everyone's astrological sign is different from the claims of the newspapers and books," Father Pacwa writes. "This means that everyone needs to change the astrological sign under which he or she was born. Whatever date the newspaper gives for your sign, move it back one whole sign, because that, in fact, is your real sign."[178]

A basis in pseudoscience is just one of the problems associated with astrology. Resorting to this form of divination can open doors to the occult.

"In principle, demons only intervene when they are invoked," writes the exorcist Father Jose Marie Fortea. "Forms of guessing the future such as horoscopes and tarot cards do not call upon 'hidden powers' or unknown spiritual beings; as such, they are not demonic. They are merely superstitious practices. But

---

[178] "The Future is Reserved for God: Pope John Paul the Great on Astrology," *Zenit News*, January 12, 2002

those who practice such superstitions open themselves up to the temptation to invoke such powers and unknown beings."[179]

This was the case with Marcia Montenegro, a former professional astrologer who once engaged in occult activities until returning to her Christian faith.

"When reading astrological charts, I did on occasion receive startlingly accurate information that seemed to be fed into my mind. I usually went into an altered state of consciousness and felt a beam of energy connect me to the chart (not the client)."[180]

This connection with the occult is why reading horoscopes, even just for kicks, is a bad idea. "Even though millions of people follow horoscopes with greater or lesser interest, this is still a type of fortune telling," writes the Most Reverend Donald W. Montrose, Bishop of Stockton, California. "Even if you say you do not believe in horoscopes, and only read your own for fun, you should abandon this practice. The daily horoscope can easily influence us from time to time. It is a way in which we open ourselves to the occult."[181]

Instead, the faithful are urged to put their trust in God's providence rather than in the dubious readings of stargazers.

"If we want to give good direction to our life, we must learn to discern its plan, by reading the mysterious 'road signs' God puts in our daily history," St. John Paul II said during an Angelus address in 1998. "For this purpose neither horoscopes nor fortune-telling is useful. What is needed is prayer, authentic prayer, which should always accompany a life decision made in conformity with God's law."[182]

---

179 *Interview with an Exorcist*, pg. 114
180 Montenegro, Marcia "I See Dead People: A Look at After-Death Communication," accessed on Christian Answers to the New Age website
181 Montrose, Donald W., D.D. *Spiritual Warfare: The Occult Has Demonic Influence*, Pastoral Letter, (Washington, NJ, AMI Press)
182 St. John Paul II, Angelus Address, September 6, 1998

Aura Reading

An aura is a kind of glow emitted from the body that is produced by a very low level of electricity known as an electromagnetic field. Clairvoyants and other New Age enthusiasts claim to be able to read or scan auras in order to diagnose illness, affect healing, predict the future, determine a person's temperament, etc. They either do this with their natural vision - a feat no one has ever successfully demonstrated - or with their "inner" or psychic vision. These auras can appear in photographs taken by a specific method known as Kirlian photography. Occult enthusiasts claim this glow is generated by the inner spirit or "life force" of the person.

However, according to Victor Stenger, Ph.D., professor emeritus of Physics and Astronomy at the University of Hawaii, there is nothing mysterious about the human aura. It is comprised of "black body" electromagnetic radiation which produces an invisible infrared light that is the result of the random movements of all the charged particles in the body that are caused by heat.

"The type of light that is emitted from a living body has a characteristic shape that is completely specified by the body's absolute temperature," he writes. "As that temperature rises, you can begin to see the aura...It is as featureless as it can be and still be consistent with the laws of physics. Any fanciful shapes seen in photographed auras can be completely attributed to optical and photographic effects. The auras are unrelated to any property of the body that one might identify as 'live' rather than 'dead' and the tendency for people to see patterns where none exist."[183]

Automatic Writing

Automatic writing is used to receive messages from deceased persons or demons masquerading as other discarnate entities through writing. The practitioner holds a writing

---

183 Stenger, Victor, "The Energy Fields of Life," *Skeptical Inquirer*, June 1, 1998

instrument which begins to move independently across the page and writes out messages.

Automatic writing is also known as trance writing because the person goes into a kind of trance and writes whatever comes to mind very quickly and without forethought. New Agers believe this allows a person to tap into the subconscious mind where the "true self" exists and where deep and mystical thoughts can be accessed. Others use automatic writing to access outside "intelligences" and spiritual entities for advice and guidance.

There are many famous automatic writers, such as Jane Roberts, a psychic and spirit medium who claimed to be channeling a spirit named Seth who imparted all the wisdom of the universe to her which she shared with the rest of the world in a series of best-selling books. Roberts and her husband met Seth while playing with a Ouija board and eventually abandoned the board and took up pen and paper to continue their dialogue. Roberts' husband even painted a picture of Seth, which the entity claimed was a very good rendition of himself. During these sessions with Seth, the entity would take control of Jane and she would speak aloud while her husband wrote down everything she said.

Helen Schucman, a prominent psychologist who once taught the famous Franciscan psychologist Father Benedict Groeschel, authored *A Course in Miracles* while she was supposedly channeling Jesus Christ. The book is riddled with theological errors and attempts to dismantle the Judeo-Christian perspective in order to replace it with a New Age worldview. Schucman insisted that Jesus dictated the book to her over the course of seven years, describing His voice as being "...strictly mental ... otherwise I would consider it hallucinatory activity."[184]

Another popular book, *God Calling*, was written by two "listeners" in the 1930s who were practicing automatic writing when they supposedly received direct messages from Our Lord. One of the listeners explains that in 1932, she received a copy of a book by A. J. Russell entitled, *For Sinners Only*, and was so

---

184 *A Course in Miracles*, www.acim.org

impressed she and a friend decided one day to "get guidance" from the Lord in the way A. J. Russell recommends in the book.

Russell's method involves sitting down with paper and pencil, letting the mind go blank, then writing down anything that flashes across it, which Russell says should be considered akin to God's orders for the day.

This is precisely what the two listeners did. "We sat down, pencils and paper in hand and waited.... My results were entirely negative.... But with my friend a very wonderful thing happened. From the first, beautiful messages were given to her by our Lord Himself, and every day from then these messages have never failed us."[185]

After they had a collection of these messages, they sent them to A. J. Russell who immediately got to work preparing them for publication in the book now known as *God Calling*. It's been a bestseller ever since.

It's important to note that the Vatican condemned A. J. Russell's method of communicating with God which was also being practiced by a group known as The Oxford Group/Moral Rearmament, which claimed to be a worldwide "organism" dedicated to founding a "new world order for Christ the King."[186]

Protestant authorities are equally condemning of the kind of false guidance being presented as God's words by A. J. Russell and the listeners in *God Calling*. For example, Pastor Harold T. Commins, who had been a former member of the Oxford Group, said "this idea of 'guidance' is false to the Scriptures....Sitting down with paper and pencil in hand and letting the mind go absolutely blank and then writing down whatever flashes across the mind as God's orders for the day is beyond anything promised or sanctioned in Scripture. Indeed this 'passivity' of mind is a

---

185 Gruss, Edmund, Book Review, *Christian Research Institute Journal*, Summer 1988, Volume 11, No. 1, pg. 29
186 Vatican Documents Clarify Moral Re Armament View, *NCWC News Service*, January 19, 1961, accessed online at thecatholicnewsarchive.org

very perilous condition to be in for it is precisely at such moments that Satan gains control and does his devilish work."[187]

Sarah Young, author of the best-selling *Jesus Calling*, was enchanted by the listener's work in *God Calling* and, according to the foreword which used to appear in *Jesus Calling*, said she began to wish for the same abilities and decided to take up the same practice.

"I began to wonder if I, too, could receive messages during my times of communing with God," she wrote. "I had been writing in prayer journals for years, but that was one-way communication: I did all the talking. I knew that God communicated with me through the Bible, but I yearned for more. Increasingly, I wanted to hear what God had to say to me personally on a given day. I decided to listen to God with pen in hand, writing down whatever I believe He was saying. I felt awkward the first time I tried this, but I received a message. It was short, biblical, and appropriate. It addressed topics that were current in my life: trust, fear, and closeness to God. I responded by writing in my prayer journal."[188]

Although the reviewers of Young's work found nothing wrong with the doctrine in the alleged messages, they expressed concern over the way she infers that while the Bible is inerrant and infallible, it is not sufficient – at least not for her.

"It was not enough for her and, implicitly, she teaches that it cannot be enough for us," writes Protestant author Tim Challies. "After all, it was not reading Scripture that proved her most important spiritual discipline, but this listening, this receiving of messages from the Lord. It is not Scripture she brings to us, not primarily anyway, but these messages from Jesus."[189]

His ultimate recommendation is that *Jesus Calling* is, in its own way, a very dangerous book. "Though the theology is largely sound enough, my great concern is that it teaches that

---

187 Book Review, *Christian Research Institute Journal*
188 Quoted by Challies, Tim, in "10 Serious Problems with Jesus Calling," November 11, 2015, accessed at Challies.com
189 Challies, Tim, "Jesus Calling," July 12, 2011, accessed at *Challies.com*

hearing words directly from Jesus and then sharing these words with others is the normal Christian experience. In fact, it elevates this experience over all others. And this is a dangerous precedent to set. I see no reason that I would ever recommend this book."[190]

Young's emulation of the two listeners from *God Calling* caused so much controversy that the publisher, Thomas Nelson, eventually deleted all mention of this connection from later editions of the book.

ESP/Telepathy

All people have psychic ability to some extent, but there is a vast difference between what is known as normal ESP (extrasensory perception) and occult ESP.

"Normal ESP is the ability to know of an event while it is in process, a telepathic capacity to access information simultaneously present in another person's mind. This normal form of ESP has nothing to do with the occult. It is a latent sense often referred to as a *sixth sense* or *intuition*, more developed in some people, most likely present in all."[191]

Normal ESP is what occurs when a mother instinctively knows that an absent child is in danger, or when a couple who has been married for many years seems to be able to "read each other's minds."

Whereas normal ESP comes without invitation or seeking, occult ESP involves deliberate attempts to use these powers to acquire knowledge.

"The key element distinguishing normal ESP from occult ESP is the *source* of the knowledge. Does it originate from a link to a human mind or from a link to the mind of an interdimensional being, identified biblically as a demon?"[192]

---

190 Ibid
191 *Kingdom of the Occult*, pg. 227
192 Ibid, pg. 227-228

There are three main categories of occult ESP, clairvoyance (perceiving events beyond normal sensory contact), precognition (foreknowledge of an event), and mediumship (mediating communication between spirits of the dead and the living), all of which glean information from demonic sources.

In addition to these practices, psychic phenomena can also include levitation, which is "the ability of a solid object to defy the laws of gravity and rise up from the earth with no visible means of support."[193]

Levitation frequently occurs during seances when objects or people rise off the floor by a means not visible to observers.

Apportation (telekinesis) is similar in that it involves the movement of objects and even people from one place to another without visible means.

Materialization (apparition) occurs when a spirit takes on a physical form and makes itself visible.

Psychic healing, another form of occult ESP, involves persons who believe they have the power to heal psychically and without physical interventions. The psychic Edgar Cayce (1877-1945) was perhaps the most famous healer who was able to diagnose people's medical conditions from hundreds of miles away.

Psychic surgeons take it one step further. Although mostly scam artists, they claim to be able to treat patients without anesthesia and often appear to reach inside a person and remove the disease from the body. The most recent case of a high-profile psychic healer from Brazil named John of God (João Teixeira de Faria) who was accused of sexually abusing women, is an example of the many dangers associated with frequenting these "healers." During his practice, de Faria claimed to be channeling 30 "doctor entities" and would employ a variety of "carnival tricks" to allegedly cure ailments as serious as cancer and malignant tumors. None of his cures were ever scientifically validated.

---

193 Ibid, pg. 233

Psychic prediction, such as the prophecies of the respected astrologer and court physician, Nostradamus (d. 1566), is another example of the use of occult ESP. Even though many of his prophecies appeared to have come true, "not a single quatrain Nostradamus wrote was interpreted or understood *before* it came to pass," writes Walter Martin in *Kingdom of the Occult*. "Since clairvoyance is connected to the occult, and Nostradamus was admittedly involved in it, it should come as no surprise that some of his predictions might be fulfilled. His accuracy overall, however, remains a hit-or-miss proposition, the hallmark of occult prophecy. In contrast, the biblical prophets of God maintained 100 percent accuracy."[194]

Astral projection is another type of occult ESP. It is an out-of-body experience founded in Theosophy, a religion based on Hinduism that was founded by the infamous occultist, Madame Blavatsky. Blavatsky posited that the astral body is one of seven bodies that we all possess – one for each of the seven planes of reality. In astral projection, the astral body, which Blavatsky claims is the seat of feeling and desire, leaves the physical body and is able to travel independently. During the trip, it allegedly remains linked to the physical body by a very fine elastic silver cord.

It's one thing to rely on our natural perception, but "when people deliberately try to access ESP; they trespass willingly into the world of the occult, attempting to acquire power over an unexplainable phenomenon. Quite often, intentional exploration of paranormal power or experiences opens the heart and mind to the occult."[195]

As Walter Martin warns, "When the mind and heart are opened to these types of occult experiences, a person becomes exposed to malignant spiritual beings waiting to take advantage of any vulnerability. Astral projection may seem harmless on the surface, but its potential impact can be devastating."[196]

---

194 *Kingdom of the Occult*, pg. 243
195 Ibid, pg. 226
196 Ibid, pg. 245

New Age Movement

The New Age movement, with its pantheistic belief in a universal life force energy and its emphasis on the perfection of Self, offers plenty of temptation to the seeker of secret knowledge. From its self-help books touting the Law of Attraction to its embrace of eastern mysticism that promises instant enlightenment and the bliss of altered states, many souls have been led away from the worship of Jesus Christ.

Although most are unaware of the philosophy upon which these fads are founded, the New Age movement has very specific beliefs that are embraced, to one degree or another, by its proponents.

It is primarily pantheistic, which is a belief that all things - animate and inanimate - are God. Therefore, because God, humans and the universe are considered to be one and interconnected, everything, including us, is divine. The goal of the pantheist is to discover and unleash one's divinity which is accomplished by achieving enlightenment through practices such as yoga, mindfulness meditation, or tapping into the secrets of the universe through a variety of self-help programs such as *A Course in Miracles* and *The Secret*.

In the New Age philosophy, the only authority is the self. The New Age does not believe in the personification of evil and there is no such thing as good or evil – it's only a matter of good or bad *choices*. These beliefs, coupled with the notion that there is no such thing as sin and humans can perfect themselves through their own efforts and/or through the help of enlightened people, effectively eliminate the need for Redemption. Because they believe there is no evil and no sin, there is no need for a Savior. Therefore, Jesus Christ is relegated to a list of other prophets and "enlightened persons."

Walter Martin summed up the New Age philosophy very succinctly: "In contrast to the true God who created man in his image, the New Age philosophy re-created God in man's image and likeness."[197]

The New Age movement has always been firmly rooted in the occult. It originated with Emanuel Swedenborg (1688-1772), the son of a Swedish Lutheran minister and founder of Swedenborgianism who became a famous trance medium later in life. Swedenborg claimed to have had conversations with biblical figures such as Jesus and St. Paul from whom he acquired special knowledge.

His teachings became the basis for the nineteenth century's New England transcendentalism which so enamored the likes of Ralph Waldo Emerson and whose followers believed that the "universal soul or mind permeates creation and is the source of all knowledge, wisdom, and intuition."[198]

In the mid-nineteenth century, a medium named Andrew Jackson Davis, who laid the groundwork for modern spiritualism, claimed to have been communicating posthumously with Swedenborg. The teachings he supposedly received during these communications were incorporated into the book, *Principles of Nature* (1847), and were embraced by his followers.

They were passed on via the Universal Church of the Master in 1908 and made their way into the formation of Helena Blavatsky's Theosophical Society in 1875 which also relied upon mediumship and clairvoyance to channel the wisdom of twelve "Ascended Masters."

Around the same time, Mary Baker Eddy and her Christian Science movement, which were also influenced by Swedenborg, shaped the idea of "mind over matter" from which the New Thought movement was born. The New Thought movement, from which today's New Age Movement evolved, promotes the idea of self-healing through "mental science."

The influx of eastern mysticism into what would become today's New Age movement began in 1893 when Swami

---

[197] *Kingdom of the Occult*, pg 193
[198] Ibid, pg. 200

Vivekananda spoke at the 1893 World Parliament of Religions event in Chicago and intrigued Westerners with the tenets of eastern religions.

Later, a yogi named Paramahansa Yogananda came to the U.S. and taught about the latent occult powers of the third eye while promoting yoga and meditation. This influx of eastern mysticism into the New Age movement would continue into the 1960s with the erection of Zen centers that furthered the spread of these practices throughout the United States.

Added to this mix of occult practices was that of Alice Bailey, who promoted occult mediumship including channeling and telepathy. She founded Lucifer's Trust (now known as Lucis Trust), an organization that bills itself as being "dedicated to the establishment of a new and better way of life for everyone in the world based on the fulfillment of the divine plan for humanity."[199]

These practices all evolved into what we know today as the New Age movement which came to life during the rebellious 1960s. It was during this time that a young Stanford University graduate named Michael Murphy, who studied at the Sri Aurobindo Ashram in Pondicherry, India, founded the Esalen Institute at Big Sur, California. Murphy, along with fellow Stanford alumnus Dick Price, created the Human Potential Movement with its focus on advancing the potentials of human nature and raising man's consciousness in order to form a better human race.[200] These efforts shaped today's self-help movement, an integral part of the New Age, and inspired works such as *A Course in Miracles, Dianetics* (Scientology), Silva Mind Control, Rebirthing, and hundreds more, all of which promote a human-centered psychology based on the belief that a person is in complete control of their destiny.

The Pontifical document, *Jesus Christ, the Bearer of the Water of Life*, referred to the Human Potential Movement as "the

---

199 Lucis Trust website
200 Esalen Institute website

clearest example of the conviction that humans are divine, or contain a divine spark within themselves."[201]

This movement also saw the explosion of energy-based practices such as Reiki, Therapeutic Touch, reflexology, homeopathy, crystal therapy, iridology and many more. All of these practices are founded upon the notion of a universal life force energy (chi, qi, prana, vital force, etc.) which remains unsubstantiated by science. Reliance on this energy for healing, health, and well-being instead of the providence of God is why the Church refers to it as "the New Age god."[202]

With this kind of history, it's no surprise that today's New Age movement embraces everything from astrology, divination, and necromancy, to parapsychology, mediumship, channeling and a variety of ancient pagan practices such as Druidism and shamanism.

"The New Age movement today must be recognized for what it is: the ancient world of the occult presented in new terminology."[203]

From its very beginning, the New Age sought to undermine Christianity because it was seen as a barrier to the advancement of its godless philosophies.

"Part of the New Age success came from undermining Christianity and destroying God's revelation - the Bible. This was important from their viewpoint, since most of these groups believed that man was in the process of evolving from his current status to yet a higher being. Darwinian evolution was part of their process, and since a large number of evangelical Christians still believed in man as God's special creation, Christianity was seen as a blockade to their movement."[204]

---

[201] Pontifical Council for Culture, Pontifical Council for Interreligious Dialogue, *Jesus Christ the Bearer of the Water of Life: A Christian Reflection on the New Age*, 2003, Section 4
[202] Ibid
[203] *Kingdom of the Occult*, pg. 199
[204] Ibid, pg 190

Numerology

Numerology is another form of divination that uses numbers to interpret a person's character or to predict the future.

According to the *Encyclopedia of Occultism and Parapsychology*, there are several different kinds of numerology that are used for divination purposes.

Gemantria, from the Greek word geometria, assigns numbers to each letter in the Hebrew alphabet in order to reveal a deeper, alternative or hidden meaning in the words. For instance, in Genesis 42:2 when Jacob tells his sons to "go down" to purchase grain in Egypt, the words "go down" in Hebrew equal 210. This is interpreted by the numerologist to mean that Israel's sojourn will last 210 years.

Modern numerology was developed by a fortune teller named Cheiro (Count Louis Hamon) who developed a system of what he called "fadic" numbers, which were arrived at by adding together all the digits in the subject's birth date to produce a "number of destiny" to which special planetary and other significance was then attached.

"In general, numerology systems assign numerical values to the letters of one's name and/or birthplace. These are added together to ascertain a basic number, which has a special symbolic interpretation, much as astrological types are traditionally assigned particular characteristics of helpful and harmful influences. Sometimes lucky or unlucky numbers are also related to the 22 symbols of the major arcana of the Tarot pack."[205]

The belief that the numbers such as 11:11 have some kind of mystical meaning is linked to numerology. There are many New Age and occult-based theories about these particular numbers, such as the belief that the number 11 is a "master number" and when paired with another 11 means one's "spirit guides" are trying to contact them. Others say it's a sign of spiritual awakening or a

---

[205] *Encyclopedia of Occultism and Parapsychology*, pg. 1127

confirmation that a person is on the right path. Still others believe 11:11 is a sign that angels are near.

A big proponent of 11:11 sightings is Uri Geller, the Israeli illusionist, magician, and self-proclaimed psychic. He has also experienced frequent 11:11 sightings and explains on his blog: "I believe that people who have constant contact with the 1111 phenomena have some type of a positive mission to accomplish. It is still a mystery to me what it is that we all have to do or why are we all being gathered and connected together, but it is very real and tangible, I feel that it is immensely positive, almost like there is a thinking entity sending us these physical and visual signs from the universe. In me, it activates the power of prayer, love and determination to somehow help the world. Someday I suspect we will find out the true meaning behind this puzzling phenomenon. It could start happening to you too after reading my website."[206]

All of these beliefs are based in superstition.

The use of numbers to predict the future, or as a sign from a supernatural power that is not sourced in God, is strictly forbidden by the Church.

Ouija Board

Far from a harmless game, some exorcists say that 90 percent of their worst cases involving demonic activity have been linked to the use of the Ouija board.[207]

The game consists of an oblong piece of wood or cardboard with letters of the alphabet inscribed in a half-moon along the edge. A small heart-shaped object called a planchette is placed on top of it. Participants lightly place their fingertips on the planchette, ask questions, and then let unknown spirits spell out the answers by

---

206 Geller, Uri, "Are your eyes attracted to 11.11?" Urigeller.com
207 Catholic Answers Staff, "Is the Ouija Board Harmless?" Q&A Forum, accessed on the website

moving the planchette across the alphabet. It is typically used to contact spirits, including those of the dead.[208]

The concept of a Ouija board was born in the 19th century in Hydesville, New York with the infamous Fox sisters who sparked national interest with claims they had successfully contacted a dead peddler. The girls would ask the peddler questions, then call out letters of the alphabet and wait for a rapping sound to confirm the letter. Although it was eventually discovered that the girls were playing an elaborate game, the idea of divining the future by asking the dead to spell words became a popular new novelty. In 1890, two U.S. businessmen named Elijah Bond and Charles Kennard patented the idea of using a planchette and alphabet board which they called a "talking board." While some believe the board received the name "Ouija" by combining the French *oui* for "yes," and the German, "ja" which also means "yes," researchers say it was a medium named Helen Peters, who was Bond's sister-in-law, who supplied the name.

"Sitting around the table, they asked the board what they should call it; the name "Ouija" came through and, when they asked what that meant, the board replied, 'Good luck.' Eerie and cryptic—but for the fact that Peters acknowledged that she was wearing a locket bearing the picture of a woman, the name 'Ouija' above her head," explains Smithsonian Magazine.[209]

As it turns out, the woman in the locket was actually named Ouida, not Ouija, but the misread name stuck.

This was the beginning of one of the most popular – albeit dangerous - "toys" of all time. It was directly linked to the most famous case of a young boy living in the Pacific Northwest who became possessed after trying to summon the spirit of his dead aunt with a Ouija board. This case became the basis for the blockbuster movie, *The Exorcist*.

---

208 Ankerberg, John and Dr. John Weldon, "The Ouija Board," published on the website in 2003
209 McRobbie, Linda Rodriquez, "The Strange and Mysterious History of the Ouija Board," *Smithsonian Magazine,* October 27, 2013

The board, which comes in several versions designed particularly for children, has remained among the top-selling games almost since its creation.

"People, especially young people and teenagers who are likely to experiment with Ouija boards on a whim, can be very naive in thinking that they are only contacting the departed souls of loved-ones when they attempt to communicate with the dead using the boards," said a priest from Dublin, Ireland. "... But it does leave people open to all kinds of spiritual dangers. People don't intend any spiritual harm by it, but we live in a spiritual realm and you have no way to control what may impinge on you."[210]

A spinoff of the Ouija board, known as the Charlie Charlie Challenge, was wildly popular with teens on social media in 2015. Some versions of the game require two pencils to be laid on a piece of paper in the shape of a cross with the words "yes" and "no" written on the paper. The players then repeat the phrase, "Charlie, Charlie can we play?" in order to summon the spirit of an alleged dead child named Charlie.

If Charlie decides to answer, he moves the pencils to indicate whether he's in the mood for play or not. If he does want to "play", participants can then ask questions which he answers by moving the pencils to either "yes" or "no", similar to how a Ouija board works. To end the game, both players must chant, "Charlie, Charlie, can we stop?" After the pencils move, both players must drop their pencils on the floor which they believe breaks contact with the spirit.

Teens who played the game reported a variety of paranormal activities associated with it, such as hearing voices, sinister laughter, objects moving around, etc.

The Spanish exorcist, Father Jose Marie Fortea called the game dangerous and warned that "...some spirits who are at the root of that practice will harass some of those who play the game." While not risking outright possession, participants in this

---

[210] "'Ouija boards can release evil spirits,' says priest," *Christian News*, December 1, 2014

game can expect that the spirits they invoke "will stay around for a while" in spite of the rules which say the spirit has to leave when the game is done.[211]

Participants also risk that playing the game "will result in other spirits beginning to enter into even more frequent communication," he warned. "And so then the person really can suffer much worse consequences from the demons" who are pretending to be "Charlie."[212]

Psychics

A psychic, also known as a soothsayer, is a person who acts as a medium but does not necessarily contact the dead. Instead, their preferred methods of divination involve the use of clairvoyance, the reading of auras, telepathy, numerology, runes, etc. as a means of acquiring unknown information to a person.

A clairvoyant is someone who claims to be able to discern facts about a person by "seeing" them much like watching a motion picture. "This is the practice of seeing things that other people do not naturally see. Usually this comes through dreams, visions, or precognition."[213]

A clairaudient is able to "hear" things that are otherwise inaudible.

A clairsentient makes predictions via insights or a sudden influx of knowledge.

One former clairvoyant, Catholic author and public speaker, Moira Noonan, explained the different kinds of psychic abilities in her book, *Ransomed from Darkness*.

"A clairvoyant is someone who can see into the past, present or future. This is different from a psychic who is clairaudient, one

---
[211] "Is 'Charlie, Charlie' a harmless game? Exorcist says absolutely not," Catholic News Agency, May 27, 2015
[212] Ibid
[213] *Kingdom of the Occult*, pg. 196

who gets information by hearing or a clairsentient, one who does so by feeling. I received information by seeing, which means I saw movies playing in my mind. When someone came to me for psychic counseling, I could see events of their life flashing before me and know many things about them - personal things." [214]

The psychic generally offers a client advice or "tips" about the future and recommends a course of action based upon their revelations. Not surprising, the psychic business is rife with sham artists who use tricks such as hot and cold reading to make their abilities appear genuine.

For example, popular stage psychics may employ a tactic known as cold reading which is gleaning information from the way people act, speak, dress, etc. and use high probability guesses about the nature of their client. In hot reading, people disguised as missionaries or door-to-door salesmen are sent into neighborhoods where the show is being televised to glean information about the prospective audience.

Not all psychic revelations are the result of clever cheating, however. Some psychics do receive information from satanic sources. Even though Satan cannot foretell the future, as Pope Benedict XVI said about prophecy, "the devil cannot of his own natural knowledge foretell future events which are the proper objects of prophecy, yet God may make use of him for this purpose."[215]

This is why Msgr. Leon Cristiani, French priest and author of *Evidence of Satan in the Modern World*, believes that attempts to foretell the future outside of the realm of divinely inspired prophecy, are "satanic in the sense that is an encroachment on the divine."[216]

---

214 Noonan, Moira, *Ransomed From Darkness* (El Sobrante, CA: *North Bay Books,* 2003), p 38
215 *Angels and Devils*, pg. 280, quoting the *Catholic Encyclopedia*, Vol XII, pg. 474
216 *Evidence of Satan in the World*

Regardless of whether the psychic believes he or she is consorting with the devil while employing these nefarious "talents," they are indeed collaborators with Satan which places themselves, and their clients, in great danger.

Runes

Runes are popularly used in the occult arts of divination and magic and are derived from an ancient Germanic alphabet that was used throughout Europe, Iceland and Scandinavia before the advent of the Latin alphabet. They consist of a set of 24 alphabetic symbols that are inscribed on wood, glass or stones and are usually kept in a pouch. Typically, the stones are tossed toward the sun or on an East-West axis on a white cloth.

"After casting the stones onto the cloth the ones which have fallen to the right side up are read and depending upon whether the rune is reversed or not will have a bearing upon its meaning and the reading as a whole."[217]

Each symbol has its own meaning and interpretation. For example, one stone that looks similar to the letter "F" can mean abundance and material gain, but if it appears in the reverse position, it can mean disappointment and loss.

Books are used to help in the interpretation of the runes, such as the popular *Book of Runes* by Ralph Blum.

"I suggest that each of us is an Oracle, and when you consult the Runes you are consulting your own deep knowing," Blum said. "I am committed to the premise that the Oracle will show me what constitutes right action in literally any situation."[218]

He also believes that they are useful in communicating with absent friends, including the deceased.

---

217 "Runic Magic and Divination," Crystalinks
218 Cecala, Tony, "Interview with Ralph Blum author Book of Runes," *Holistic Networker*, December 21, 2008

Spiritualism (Contacting the Dead)

One of the most serious and dangerous forms of attempting to acquire knowledge of the future is through the practice of necromancy (contacting the dead). This is a special mode of divination through the evocation of the dead. The name necromancy is derived from the old form of the name, nigromancy (niger meaning black) which suggests it to be a form of black magic in which the workings of evil spirits are present.

Scripture is full of references to the evils of this practice. "Let there not be found among you anyone who causes their son or daughter to pass through the fire, or practices divination, or is a soothsayer, augur, or sorcerer, or who casts spells, consults ghosts and spirits, or seeks oracles from the dead. Anyone who does such things is an abomination to the Lord."[219]

Despite this very clear condemnation, famous mediums and television stars such as Teresa Caputo, known as *The Long Island Medium*, who calls herself a practicing Catholic, have made this practice seem like an act of compassion toward the grieving rather than what it is – a grave sin.

The most common way to practice necromancy is through the séance which is usually comprised of two or more people sitting together in a room for the express purpose of contacting the dead. Normally, the séance will be conducted by a medium or channel, a person who acts as a conduit and allows the alleged dead spirit to speak through them. Some mediums are assisted by several spirit guides or a main spirit known as a 'control.'

The seance usually begins with someone calling for protection by asking to be surrounded by white light or a protective spirit. The medium then summons the spirit of the deceased loved one or any spirit interested in making contact.

---

219 Deut 18:10

"During a séance, a medium falls into a different state of consciousness or trance. He or she then communicates messages from beings outside of the dimension of earth."[220]

Many mediums sincerely believe that they are making contact with the actual dead; however, this merely reveals their lack of knowledge about the spiritual realm, the beings that are known to inhabit it, and the way in which these beings interact with man.

We know from Scripture, Tradition, and history in general that there are four types of spiritual beings that inhabit the spiritual world: God, angels, disembodied human souls and demons.

The disembodied human soul is what a man becomes after he dies. Once disembodied, the only way for a soul to communicate or materialize is through assistance from a being that has the capacity to provide this materialization.

This is because "part of being a physical and spiritual creature means that we use our physical bodies to communicate with physical creatures on earth. Humans have no natural power, either in this life or in the next, to communicate with the material world apart from their bodies. Any such ability would have to come from either a preternatural source (an angel or a demon) or a supernatural source (God Himself)."[221]

We know from Revelation that while God allows the dead to appear to man and facilitates it on occasion, He would never do so at the bidding of a medium. This is because He is quite explicit in condemning this practice in Scripture. For example, in Deuteronomy 18:10 we're told that those who contact the dead are "an abomination to Him" and in Leviticus 19:31 we're warned not to turn to ghosts or consult spirits because we will be "defiled" by them.

---

220 *Kingdom of the Occult*, pg. 319
221 Algaier, Father Robert, "The Ouija Board: A Game or a Gamble?" *Envoy Magazine*, May/June, 2000

If God will not assent to facilitating the appearance of a disembodied soul to a medium, is it possible that one of His angels might facilitate this appearance? No, because Scripture tells us that these pure spiritual beings exist solely to serve God. "With their whole being, angels are servants and messengers of God."[222] In other words, if God will not associate with a medium, neither will His angels.

If God will not facilitate the appearance of the dead to a medium, or allow His angels to do so, and if disembodied spirits are incapable of communicating without assistance, there is only one being left which has both the power and the motive to do this – the devil.

Evil spirits have both the power and the motive to answer human attempts to communicate with the spiritual world through divination.

"Once we realize this, it becomes much easier to see why evil spirits want to communicate with humans through divination and encourage its use," Father Allgaier writes.[223]

These truths are either unknown, or ignored, by mediums, much to their own peril. This is why St. Augustine taught that the spirits who appear to mediums " ... are deceivers, not by nature, but by malice. They make themselves *gods* and *souls of the departed,* but they do not make themselves devils for they really are so."[224]

This truth is understood by exorcists to this day. "...[T]hese evoked spirits, if they are not the result of banal tricks, are none other than demons."[225]

Some like to escape this truth by claiming that some spirits are "good" because they are ascended masters or avatars or souls who are in a stage of reincarnation or "wandering" between heaven and earth. "All of this, of course, is completely contrary

---

222 *The Catechism of the Catholic Church, No.* 329
223 "The Ouija Board: A Game or a Gamble?"
224 Quoted in The Devil, pg. 97-98
225 *An Exorcist Explains the Demonic,* pg. 51

to Christian doctrine," we're told by Father Amorth. "There are no good spirits other than angels and no bad spirits other than demons."[226]

Now that we have learned about the enormous powers of the devil, it's easy to see how imitating someone's deceased relative is not in the least bit difficult for evil spirits. The devil can easily counterfeit a person's appearance, mannerisms, handwriting, even secret nuances known only to their loved ones.

"Undoubtedly, the supposed dead bring pretended proofs of their identity, but these proofs are no wise conclusive. They remind you of peculiarities which the dead and you alone knew; the mysterious pencil imitates his writing: all that may be. But the devils were invisible witnesses of those peculiarities…"[227]

The fact that the spirits of the dead do appear to the faithful from time to time, such as in the apparitions of the saints, is a source of confusion for the faithful who do not realize the distinction between *invocation* and *evocation* of the dead.

As the exorcist Father Francesco Bamonte explains, when we pray for the intercession of the dead, we are *invoking* the dead, which means we are calling upon them for help. What spiritualists do is *evoke* the dead, which means they provoke normally invisible spirits to appear.

"The dead can only manifest themselves to us by the free initiative of God, directly and never through techniques or mediums such as spiritualistic séances. For serious reasons, God can allow a dead person to appear to us, for example, to give us advice or at least a consoling presence, to ask for prayers or to express gratitude for prayers offered."[228]

There are definite ways to discern whether or not a spirit is appearing through an initiative of God or through diabolical means.

---

226 Ibid, page 50
227 Ibid, pg 99
228 *Interview with an Exorcist*

As Adam Blai explains, "Human spirit manifestations are non-destructive and limited to the communication of a need for help. Human spirits may also be allowed to convey some specific wrong they did that needs to be righted, if there is a specific need beyond general prayer."[229]

These souls do not attack religious objects or produce manifestations that terrify, nor do they attack a person physically. Instead, their presence is subtle such as in the sound of a person walking or tapping on a wall. If they appear, they tend to remain silent and convey their desire for prayer by a sad or distressed look.

"If something claims to be a human soul and wants to have a conversation, answer questions, or deepen a relationship, it is a demon,"[230] writes Blai.

This is because, "The souls in purgatory are aware of God's prohibition about seeking information from the dead and so would never draw the living into this sin by casual communication beyond a need for help."[231]

On the other hand, spirits of darkness often produce negative physical effects ranging from strong stomach pains, pains in the forehead and bones, vomiting, epileptic fits, pins and needles in the legs, to sudden attacks of heat or cold, increasing sense of anxiety, depressions, constant nervous tics, and being unable to eat.

Father Bamonte adds: "There are still many more... The inability to sleep night or day, inability to study or work. To be agitated, to have nightmares, to be afraid of the dark, to have sensations of being grabbed by the arms, or the sensation of someone sitting on our lap. One also feels invisible slaps and bites, as well as blows to the body."[232]

---

229 *Possession, Exorcism and Hauntings*, pg. 45
230 Ibid, pg. 11
231 Ibid, pg. 46
232 "Interview with an Exorcist: Father Francesco Bamonte" *Zenit*, November 4, 2003

This can also be accompanied by other phenomena such as becoming anti-social or addicted to drugs or alcohol. Others report feelings of being possessed by another personality and/or hearing voices that blaspheme and/or lead to suicide.

Perhaps the best evidence that spirits contacted through spiritualism are evil can be found in their messages. "Note that the messages from the 'dead,' from the spirits, and from channeled entities never encourage people to believe the Bible, never urge people to trust Christ for salvation, and often openly contradict God's word or even speak derisively of Christ as Savior."[233]

Spiritists themselves warn others to stay away. Father Herbert Thurston, author of *Butler's Book of Saints* who spent years studying the paranormal, writes about Mrs. Travers Smith, one of London's most respected mediums, who did not hesitate to warn anyone who would listen against the practice of contacting the dead. Once plagued by a spirit of suicide who repeatedly tried to possess her, she warns people to never attempt spirit communication, especially not lightly or for fun.

"You will draw to yourself earth-bound and still evil spirits ... mischievous messages will follow and oft-times actual mental damage to yourself."[234]

Rarely do these spirits speak the truth anyway, Father Thurston learned. After compiling years of study on the subject, he concluded that the overwhelming majority of spirits who speak to the living are "freakish or impersonating spirits," or what he calls "silly spirits" who deliberately mislead people.

Apparently, there are vast minions of these spiritual clowns, he says, who for "pure sportive fun frequent circles, counterfeit manifestations, assume names and give erroneous and misleading information... . And yet, it is through channels such as these that spiritualists bid us seek the solution of the most profound mysteries of man's existence and destiny."[235]

---

233 Montenegro, Marcia "Spirit Contact: Who is on the Other Side?"
234 Thurston, Herbert, *The Church and Spiritualism*, p. 93
235 Ibid, p. 99

Tarot Cards

The use of tarot cards is the most serious form of divination by cards. Commonly used by mediums and psychics to predict the future, the use of tarot cards is also linked with magic, numerology, astrology and other practices. In the present day, tarot cards are used for both divination as well as to cultivate intuition and psychic ability. Practitioners believe that when laying out the cards, they will fall into positions that inevitably relate to the subject of the reading.

The typical tarot deck is comprised of 78 cards which are divided into the Major and Minor Arcana. The Minor Arcana is made up of 56 cards which are divided into four suits – Pentacles, Wands, Cups, and Swords – which are usually linked to the four elements of earth, air, water and fire. The Major Arcana has 22 cards containing symbolic pictures such as The Emperor, The Tower, Death, The Devil, etc. These cards are said to represent the legends, myths, philosophies, religions and magic beliefs of the human race.

"There are many different ways of consulting the cards for divination, but they mostly involve laying out the cards after shuffling and interpreting the indications of the major symbolic cards in their relationship to each other."[236]

The use of these cards has been associated with demonic infestations, such as the case of an ex-tarot card reader known only as Tina who shared her witness with the New Age Deception website.[237]

Tina converted to Christianity and repented of her occult involvement. No sooner had she given up her cards when she began to be stalked by a dark spirit.

---

[236] Tarot (or Tarots), *Encyclopedia of Occultism and Parapsychology*, (Farmington, MI: *Gale Group*) 5th Edition, pg. 1533

[237] "Danger of the Tarot Cards – Testimony of Tina an ex tarot-card reader," New Age Deception, June 6, 2019

"I started to feel a presence which kept coming to me, very often, almost weekly. It came at any time, out shopping, at work, sitting on a bus, when I was fully awake. I guess it was because I had finally broken the connection, and it was trying to keep it," Parker said.[238]

At first, she wasn't afraid of the presence, but it gradually grew stronger and more menacing. "As the weeks went by, it became stronger, and in its presence I could feel it's energy blending more with mine, my body felt quite heavy, I began to feel incredibly nauseous when it was around and my mind felt 'spaced out.'"[239]

Finally, while at a church gathering, the presence made her feel as if it was trying to take control of her, that she was speaking and singing and participating, but that it "wasn't quite me."

Thankfully, the presence left her and did not return, but it was an experience she never forgot. "I realized afterwards this was the beginnings of something wanting to take possession of my faculties. This was the beginnings of something evil forcing me into trance against my will."[240]

The use of tarot or any other card to foresee the future is strictly forbidden by the Church.

These examples of divination, which are so popular today, are all part of an age-old heresy known as Gnosticism, which is the reliance upon secret wisdom or knowledge instead of upon salvation by Jesus Christ. In today's increasingly secular world, it is considered hip to divine the future, to tap into mysterious life force energies, to discern our inner divinity, or become one with the universe. Meanwhile, beneath the guise of what is known as "hipster occultism,"[241] Satan continues his primordial game of seduction and destruction of human souls.

---

238 Ibid
239 Ibid
240 Ibid
241 Elizondo, Joseph I. "Don't be Seduced by Hipster Occultism," *Catholic Exchange*, May 29, 2019

Chapter Four

Extraordinary Satanic Activity

"Are there signs of diabolic presence? If so, what are they?"
— *Pope St. Paul VI*

In the last two chapters, we learned about Satan's typical tactic of temptation to sin and the many ways that he uses it to lead us into sin, whether into mortal sin, or by enticing us to indulge our thirst for power or secret knowledge by participating in sinful activities. In this chapter, we will deal with extraordinary Satanic activity, which is not the devil's preferred way to act.

"…[T]he demon does not particularly like exercising his extraordinary action; he prefers by far to act through temptation," writes Father Gabriele Amorth. "In the first case, the external manifestation clearly unmasks his existence. In the second, hiding himself behind ignorance and slight faith, he can act more easily because he is undisturbed."[242]

However, when he does choose this route, he usually acts upon our human nature. Satan exploits our wounded nature, caused by Original Sin and the trials and tribulations of life, to gain a much deeper access into our lives. He does this by forming strongholds within us that he uses to exert control over us. These strongholds are formed by engaging in habitual mortal sin such as viewing pornography or dabbling in the occult. If left unchecked, these strongholds can quickly escalate into outright oppression

---

242 *An Exorcist Explains the Demonic*

or obsession that can manifest in various ways, from spiritual bondage to infestations.

Demonic oppression is described as an external attack of some kind, such as those involving a victim's finances, relationships, or employment. The dire straits of the biblical character, Job, are an example of what oppression may look like.

On the other hand, demonic obsession refers to an attack that is internal in some way, such as inspiring evil thoughts that a victim cannot stop; evil or frightening dreams; or clinging to pain of deep emotional wounds.

"All of these problems are demonic in a certain way," Father Driscoll writes, "since Satan is the primary cause of evil in the world, and his demons are always looking for ways to inflict damage on us. However, it would be a mistake to give the devil too much credit for such problems."[243]

For example, although demons can play a role in physical suffering, we should always look to health care providers first for evaluation and possible treatment.

"The bottom line is that because demons are evil and cruel, they attack all of us at our weak points."[244]

Demonic Oppression

Demonic oppression occurs after a demon has gained the right to interact with a person and begins to exercise those rights.

"Demons often develop a relationship of consent with a person, or family line, over years before it evolves into demonic oppression," writes Adam Blai. "This is because demons don't cause distress until they have enough rights to remain without the person's ongoing consent. The demons then start controlling the person through threats and punishment."[245]

---

243 *Demons, Deliverance, and Discernment*, pg. 46
244 Ibid, pg. 47
245 *Possession, Exorcism, and Hauntings*, pg. 55

One of the most common ways they go about gaining this consent is by employing a tactic known as spiritual bondage. This can occur when a person repeatedly gives into temptation which gradually becomes a sinful habit that a person clings to with affection.

As the desert Fathers taught, when a person gives into temptation, "a process is set in motion that leads to 'enslavement' or 'captivity' of the soul."[246]

This process starts with bondage. As the fifth-century monk, St. John Cassian, described: "It is clear then that unclean spirits cannot make their way into those whose bodies they are going to seize upon, in any other way than by first taking possession of their minds and thoughts...It is a fact those people are grievously and severely troubled who, while they seem to be very little affected by them in the body, are yet possessed in spirit in a far worse way, as they are entangled in their sins and lusts. For as the apostle says, 'whatever overcomes a man, to that he is enslaved' (2 Pet. 2;19). Only in this respect they are more dangerously ill, because though they are the demons' slaves, yet they do not know they are assaulted by them, and under their dominion."[247]

In spiritual bondage, the will is to some degree constrained and the conscience may not even perceive that something is wrong.

"Sin and spiritual bondage seem quite similar in that both involve the will. However, in the case of sin, the will is *divided*, whereas with bondage it is *constrained*."[248] A *divided* will may truly want the sin it is committing, but it's conscience may speak and cause it to try not to commit the sin; however, the *constrained* will is practically unable to fight. It is very similar to what traditional moral theology refers to as a vice, which is a strong tendency that becomes extremely difficult to resist. Although a

---

246 *Deliverance Ministry*, pg. 55
247 Ibid, pg. 54
248 Ibid, pg. 56

vice and spiritual bondage are not the same thing, they are very similar and often overlap and reinforce each other in real life.

However, it's important to clarify that not all vices are caused by the devil. "...[T]emptation is only temptation: demons do not and cannot *cause* sin. Most theologians agree that they cannot directly influence our mind and will, but only our imagination, emotions, the material world around us, or in some cases, our bodies. They scare or deceive or tempt us into a choice, but the choice is ours."[249]

Unlike possession, when a person, whether consciously or unconsciously, gives a demon the right to an inner control, spiritual bondage is "a milder form of this inner hold: an *influence* rather than control."[250]

While possession is extremely rare, spiritual bondage, especially in its milder forms, may touch every aspect of life. This is why Christians are encouraged to "put on the armor of God"[251] and actively engage in spiritual warfare through the exercise of the Sacraments, the use of sacramentals, and remaining close to God in prayer.

The most common types of spiritual bondage involve the emotions, our thought patterns, and our behavior.

"A first type of bondage is that of overwhelming *emotions* such as guilt, fear, jealously, despair, resentment, deep anger, rage, or hatred – sometimes directed toward a particular category of people, such as men or women, or authority figures."[252]

Another typical type involves repetitive and *obsessive thought patterns*. "For instance, there may be an attraction to death, or a habit of legalism, or a habit of interpreting the actions of others as an attack on oneself. This is sometimes related to a

---

249 *Deliverance Ministry*, pg. 46
250 Ibid, pg. 57-58
251 Ephesians 6:11
252 Ibid, pg. 59

very specific sentence or word spoken to us in the past that has an inordinate amount of influence and power in our minds."[253]

Because the mind is one of the key channels between man and God, "When Satan controls the mind, he has a strategic advantage over the direction of a person's life"[254] so this is a bond that the Evil One is most anxious to cultivate.

A third kind of bondage is known as *behavioral* bondage. "[F]or instance, an irresistible urge to isolate oneself in difficult moments, or a constant need to control situations and people. Repetitive sins and compulsory temptations, such as pornography or gambling or even lying, may fall into this category as well. In some cases, addictions can be accompanied by a demonic influence."[255] A person may also find themselves to be in bondage to a possessive or otherwise unhealthy relationship, or to an object associated with that relationship.

For the most part, spiritual bondage originates in a combination of two factors, 1) through wounds and trauma, or a psychological disorder of some kind, and 2) by consent given by the person. When these two factors are combined, Satan gains a foothold into a person's life.

His point of entry often involves *wounds and trauma* which can be caused by a painful event or series of events such as sexual, physical or emotional abuse that occurred particularly in the earlier years of life when we are the most impressionable. As a result, these circumstances create inner wounds that may lead a person to seek protection, consolation or compensation in some way that can offer an entryway for demons.

A second entry point for Satan is through repeated, unrepented *sin*, which becomes a habit that weakens the person and enables a demon to take over the will.

---

253 Ibid
254 *Deliverance from Evil Spirits*, pg. 51
255 Ibid

"Spiritual bondage then reinforces the orientation of the will toward the sin, to the point where it is incapable of choosing any other: it is not merely divided but constrained (bound)."[256]

These sins can include sins of omission, such as the refusal to forgive someone or oneself.

The third and most serious kind of entryway comes through involvement in *occult practices,* which have become alarmingly common today, even among Catholics. Playing with Ouija boards, tarot cards, dabbling in witchcraft, and astrology, along with pagan practices such as shamanism, runes, and idolatry, all open the door to Satan and his minions.

Psychological disorders can be another point of origin for spiritual bondage although it is often difficult to distinguish between spiritual bondage and psychological troubles because their symptoms can be very similar. Psychological disorders are more deeply rooted in the person's psyche and identity whereas spiritual bondage tends to affect a more limited area of a person's life.

The Church has a long tradition of carefully distinguishing between demonic affliction and mental illness. "Discernment requires prudence, wisdom, and experience."[257]

These points of entry may give Satan access to our life, but they cannot bring about spiritual bondage unless we somehow consent to it.

"Consent is not necessarily a fully conscious process. Sometimes it simply means the person embraces a judgment, however troubling, because it seems overbearingly true."[258] For example, a parent who repeatedly tells a child that they are worthless and good for nothing. Even though the child may not want to believe it, they may feel compelled to believe it is true. As a result of this forced consent, these negative comments can sink

---

256 Ibid
257 Ibid, pg. 65
258 Ibid

deep into the heart and influence thoughts and actions, perhaps leading to self-destructive behaviors later in life. This can happen even when one has embraced the truth of the Gospel. In spite of knowing better, they feel almost driven to compulsions that are rooted in these inner wounds and lies.

Another example may be someone who becomes involved in the occult practice of "automatic writing" and consents to communications with their "spirit guide" in order to gain messages which they believe will help others. Mediums who practice necromancy consent to visitations by what they believe are spirits of the dead but are actually demons who can later exert control over them even when they try to withdraw their consent.

It is through spiritual bondage that the devil keeps the soul locked inside a life of sin and darkness ranging from self-hatred and relationship ills to involvement in pornography, the occult, addiction, violence, and crime.

Demonic Vexation

Father Amorth details another type of oppression that comes in the form of what he calls "diabolical vexation." These manifestations are caused by people in bondage after cultivating many of the bad habits described above.

"Vexations are true and actual aggressions, physical or psychological attacks that the demon works against a person. At times, they result in scratches, burns, bruises, or, in the most serious cases, broken bones."[259]

These attacks can include illnesses or bodily pain with no apparent cause. Vexations can also involve psychic disturbances. In some cases, while sleeping, a victim may have terrible nightmares in which they blaspheme God or behave in perverse or wicked ways. They can affect a couple's relationship, interfere

---

259 *An Exorcist Explains the Demonic*, pg. 71

with a person's employment, or lead one to isolation from friends and family.

Father Amorth gives examples of demonic vexation in the lives of the saints, such as in Padre Pio who was often beaten by Satan in the middle of night and the Cure of Ars who frequently tangled with the devil, who he referred to as *le grappin*. This was permitted by God for the purpose of purification or reparation for sin.

The exorcist, Father Francesco Bamonte, described other examples of this kind of vexation that he witnessed in people who were involved in spiritualism, such as sensations of being grabbed by the arms, invisible slaps and bites, as well as blows to the body.[260]

Demonic Infestation

Another form of oppression comes in the form of demonic infestation. These are disturbances that typically act on houses, animals, and objects, rather than on people. They include doors and windows that open and shut without any apparent cause; lights, televisions and electronic devices that turn on and off without any human intervention; the sound of footsteps; vibrations; mysterious voices or cries; rapping sound on the walls; black shadows that float or glide along floors, walls, or ceilings; strong and revolting odors; insect invasions.

Hauntings are also a form of demonic infestation. As we learned in Chapter Three, disembodied spirits are incapable of communicating with the natural world without the intervention of either a supernatural or preternatural power. Although God does facilitate the appearance of the dead for serious reasons, He does not allow spirits to return to earth at the bidding of mediums or for the purpose of haunting a house or engaging in poltergeist activity.

---

[260] "Interview with an Exorcist: Father Francesco Bamonte," *Zenit*, November 4, 2003

As Adam Blai reports, some of the most common types of alleged human spirit haunting cases involve suicide or murder victims. "One has to be careful because demons can take advantage of a known suicide or murder and pose as that person in that location. Also, the demon that helped encourage the murder or suicide could still be there."[261]

Hauntings are also known to occur in homes where the occupants tried to communicate with the spirits of the dead, an activity that gives demons a kind of license to manifest.

In regard to these manifestations, it's important to rule out other explanations, such as the presence of living or dead animals in the walls, poor wiring that causes electrical field disturbances, noises from broken appliances or vents, and self-induced hysteria from watching too many occult-oriented horror shows on television.

The demon will often pick a particular person in the house to focus these manifestations upon in order to make it appear to other family members as if they're imagining things. Infestations may also include manifestations peculiar to vexations.

"They may scratch, bite, hit, molest and generally harm that person," writes Adam Blai. "They may invade the dreams of that person, causing unusual repeating nightmares that have an explicitly demonic character. There will be the beginning of a wearing down process, usually including sleep deprivation."[262]

The presence of evil in a house can also manifest in the form of physical discomfort such as insomnia, headaches, or stomach aches, or even just a general feeling of malaise that only happens in that particular place and nowhere else.

Father Amorth specifically mentions the reaction of house pets who seem able to sense an invisible presence that humans cannot see. "...[A] cat or a dog often fixes its eyes toward a particular

---

261 *Possession, Exorcism, and Hauntings*, pg. 47
262 *Possession, Exorcism, and Hauntings*, pg. 49-50

spot. Other times, the animals will jump up and run away in terror, as though a mysterious presence advanced on them." [263]

Poltergeist activity also falls into the category of demonic infestation and involves the movement of objects from one place to the other without any visible form of intervention. The name itself means "noisy ghost" in German. They typically manifest by moving or throwing objects around a room, stones against a window, or as moving orbs of light.

"If they succeed in catching someone's attention, they often speak to the targeted individual audibly or through digital records, Ouija boards, or automatic writing, crafting tales of tragedy and woe designed to foster sympathy in the hearts of listeners."[264]

Regardless of their sorry tales, poltergeists are demons masquerading as human souls.

"Demons enjoy playing games with human beings, and they have had centuries to perfect their technique."[265]

The *infestation of objects* is also possible, although rare. The cause is almost always a curse of some kind.

As Father Amorth explains: "In theory, every object can be cursed through a satanic rite performed by a witch doctor or anyone who has tied himself to Satan in any way. However, in reality, these occurrences are very rare..."[266]

The infestation of an object does not mean that the devil is in the object, it means that it was exposed to an evil rite and was made particularly harmful because it was meant to bring harm upon someone.

Animal infestation is also possible, although this is also very rare. Father Amorth uses the example of the pigs who

---

263 *An Exorcist Tells His Story*, pg. 124
264 *Kingdom of the Occult*, pg. 244
265 Ibid
266 *An Exorcist: More Stories*, pg. 159

were infested by a legion of demons who were cast out of the Gerasene demoniac.[267] He found that witch doctors frequently use animals for their magic rites – particularly toads and cats – and that exorcists will frequently feel the presence of invisible cats, or other animals, in a house, and actually see paw prints on the floor or find scratch marks on their bed linens.

Demonic Obsession

Where demonic oppression is usually external, demonic obsession is internal in some way.

"Diabolical obsessions are disturbances or extremely strong hallucinations that the demon imposes, often invincibly, on the mind of the victim," explains Father Amorth. "In these cases, the person is no longer master of his own thoughts. Rather, he is subjected to a powerful force that creates mental activity in him that is repetitive, obsessive, and irresistible."[268]

These hallucinations can manifest as visions, voices, rustling sounds, or as horrifying animals or devils. They can also manifest as strong impulses to suicide or to do evil to another. Other exorcists have also seen this manifestation in the young in the form of gender confusion.

"The history of cases is so vast that it is impossible to enumerate all the forms of diabolical obsession," Father Amorth writes.[269]

Even though a person is conscious and alert during these manifestations, and their mind and will are not completely overcome, they have a profound impact on the victim's relationship with the world.

---

267 Mark 5: 1-20
268 *An Exorcist Explains the Demonic*, pg. 72
269 Ibid, pg. 73

"...[E]xperiencing it can make one's life impossible, even to the point of suicide. For obvious reasons, this situation provokes sadness and desperation in the victim."[270]

Because these obsessive disturbances closely resemble mental pathologies, it is always necessary to consult with a psychiatrist in order to determine if a natural cause is to blame.

Demonic Possession

The outright possession of a human being by a demon remains rare, although there has been an increase in the number of reported cases around the world due to a general increase in participation in the occult.[271]

The most common causes of possession are involvement in Satanism, curses, and the occult with spirit communication (necromancy, Ouija, divination, etc.) being the most dangerous.

Authentic demonic possession is sometimes referred to as an analogy of the Incarnation. As Msgr. Leon Cristiani explains: "Possession is an imitation, or, as one might say, an 'aping' of the divine by Satan – a caricature of the Incarnation."[272]

In the case of a genuine possession, "the possessed person is one whose body, and even, indirectly, his spiritual faculties (except the will, which never belongs to Satan, unless with its own consent) are given up for a time to one or more devils who make him their instrument."[273]

For those who are genuinely possessed, there are certain tell-tale signs that an exorcist will look for.

First, the victim is able to speak in unfamiliar languages. "...[I]ncoherent babbling does not constitute an unfamiliar

---

[270] Ibid
[271] Stanglin, Doug, "Demand for exorcism is up three-fold in Italy, so Vatican is holding conference," *USA Today,* February 23, 2018
[272] *Evidence of Satan in the Modern World,* pg. 63
[273] *The Devil,* pg. 131

language. Exorcists are looking for a real language, whether ancient or modern."[274] For example, a priest may be performing the rite in Latin and the victim will understand exactly what he is saying even though he/she did not know the language beforehand.

Second, the victim will have knowledge of hidden events. "Blurting out information about the private life of the exorcist – or one of those assisting him – is a typical example of hidden knowledge as a sign of possession."[275]

Third, the victim exhibits extraordinary physical power that is far beyond what the individual would normally have, for example, when an otherwise frail 72-year-old woman would need five large men to restrain her during an exorcism.

The fourth sign is a negative reaction to the sacred such as shouting, physical aggression, howling, spitting, convulsing, and blaspheming when brought into the presence of the sacred.

This last sign is why the majority of persons who seek an exorcism are found to be suffering from other problems. In the case of genuine possession, it is impossible for the victim to enter a rectory and speak to a priest. Although there are some exceptions, it will almost always be the family or friends of the victim who will come looking for help. Inevitably, the possessed person will have to give his/her consent in order for an exorcism to move forward and this may be impossible due to threats from the demons. In some cases, the demons will convince the person that their suffering is "special" and willed by God because they are a "victim soul." They'll do whatever they have to in order to remain in possession of the person.

"The free will of the demoniac [victim] is central to the success of the exorcism. God does not violate free will and so one must be fully committed to choosing God and rejecting the demon," writes Adam Blai.[276]

---

274 *Demons, Deliverance, and Discernment*, pg 96
275 Ibid, pg. 97
276 *Possession, Exorcism, and Hauntings*, pg. 39

Until the person makes the decision to seek liberation, the daily life of the demoniac is one of darkness and unpredictability because the devil is not always present in the possessed but enters at will and thus provokes various "crises" in the person's life.

Father Amorth has found great diversity in the demoniacs he has treated. The strange behavior stirred up by the demon during a crisis might be as simple as a change in tone of voice or as obvious as blaspheming and cursing.

"Often demoniacs behave normally; many of them go to work, where their colleagues are oblivious of their situation. At times, however, these persons, even when they do not fall into an evident state of possession are subjected to interior assaults by the Evil One that are difficult to control. I am speaking of legs that tremble or become immobilized, of abdominal pains, headaches, sudden mood changes, and other various ailments. Thus, they learn to develop various strategies of behavior that help them to overcome the various crises without attracting too much attention; for example, going into a restroom until everything becomes normal again. There are, however, more serious cases, in which a person is impeded from having any type of professional or social life."[277]

Once a person has been determined to be possessed, and agrees to be exorcised, he/she will undergo the Rite of Exorcism which is different from what is known as deliverance.

As Father Fortea explains, "An exorcism is a liturgical rite that is carried out on people who are possessed. Deliverance is a series of private prayers prayed over people who suffer from some type of demonic influence."[278]

Deliverance is part of the charism of healing, whereas exorcism is a liturgical sacramental that can only be performed by a priest with the permission of a bishop.

---

277 *An Exorcist Explains the Demonic*, pg. 82
278 *Interview with an Exorcist*, pg. 94

It is of great importance that the faithful recognize the authority of the Church in these matters because, as Adam Blai reminds, "The spiritual world is very legalistic....The most fundamental piece of advice is the same one that was central to the fall of Lucifer: obey. Always work within the Church's authority and instruction when opposing demons. Disobeying the rules, acting on personal authority, or using methods not approved by the Church flirts with disaster."[279]

Demons themselves recognize this authority and will not only refuse commands from those who are acting outside the hierarchy of Church authority, they can choose to attack in dangerous ways.

Because of the extreme danger of direct involvement with demons, the Church has determined "that no member of the Christian faithful can use the formula of exorcism against Satan and fallen angels, extracted from that which was made law by Leo XIII, and even less are they able to use the entire text for exorcism."[280] Only an authorized priest can say the prayers of exorcism.

The Rite of Exorcism in use today is based on the Rite first promulgated by Pope Paul V in 1614 which has three parts that exorcists refer to as "Chapters" – the Instructions, the Exorcism of One Possessed by a Demon, and the Exorcism of Satan and the Fallen Angels.

The Instructions state that the exorcist must be a priest who is distinguished for his piety, prudence and integrity of life, and be well-versed on the subject. He should also exercise great discernment in determining if a person is possessed and to look for the typical signs of possession. In addition, he is told that he can take into account "various other indications which, when taken together as a whole, build up evidence of possession,"[281]

---

279 *Possession, Exorcism, and Hauntings*, pg. 30, 32
280 Congregation for the Doctrine of the Faith, *On the Current Norms Governing Exorcism*, September 29, 1985
281 *Demons, Deliverance, and Discernment*, pg. 80

an instruction which gives exorcists some latitude in making a determination.

In this section, the priest receives instructions about how to deal with demons who conceal themselves so well that even the victim is convinced that they have been delivered. A demon may even allow a person to receive the Eucharist in order to fool everyone into thinking that he has departed. However, demons are commanded during the exorcism to state the day and time of their departure and an exorcist must persist until "he sees the signs of deliverance" which have been established.

Because of Christ's words that some demons can only be driven out by prayer and fasting, the priest is also instructed to prepare for the exorcism in this way.

Exorcisms should be done in a church or some other "sacred and worthy" place if possible, and be away from crowds so as to avoid causing a sensation. However, if the person is ill, or for some other valid reason, the exorcism can take place in a private home.

He must have a crucifix, holy water, and relics of the saints if available. These can be applied to the head or breast of the person, and to sprinkle holy water and make the sign of the cross on any part of the body that swells or causes pain to the victim.

During the Rite, the priest should pay close attention to whatever words cause the evil spirits to "tremble" and to repeat them more frequently because negative reactions indicate that progress is being made.

Exorcists are also cautioned not to engage in any kind of "senseless prattle" or ask superfluous questions of the demons. "Instead, he will bid the unclean spirit keep silence and answer only when asked."[282]

However, the priest should ask necessary questions. For example, because possession typically involve numerous demons,

---

[282] Ibid, pg. 83

he should ask how many demons are inhabiting the person, the names of those demons, the time when they entered and the cause of the possession.

A single session of exorcism can range anywhere from two to four hours and even longer if there is progress.

The Rite also indicates that the exorcist should have assistants who intercede during the ritual and for restraint of the possessed if they become physically aggressive. In the case of a female victim, the exorcist should have several women of good repute with him, preferably relatives of the victim.

After the person has been freed, he is admonished to "guard himself carefully against falling into sin, so as to afford no opportunity to the evil spirit of returning, lest the last state of that man become worse than the former."[283]

The *second Chapter* explains the Rite itself.

First, the priest prepares himself by going to confession and offering Mass before the exorcism; the victim is bound in whatever way is necessary to protect him from hurting himself or the priest. The priest vests himself in a surplice and violet stole and begins by tracing the sign of the cross over the possessed person, then sprinkling him with holy water. He then kneels and recites the litany of the saints and Psalm 53 which is followed by a prayer asking God to cast out the devil.

The exorcist then demands that the demons reveal their names and the time of their departure.

This is followed by the reading of certain Gospel passages, the sprinkling of more holy water and praying for the forgiveness of the victim's sins.

The priest then makes the sign of the cross over himself and the victim, then places the end of his stole on the person's neck and his hand on his head. He says a short prayer and then

---

[283] *Demons, Deliverance, and Discernment*, pg. 86

recites the three exorcisms, each of which concludes with a prayer. While he is doing so, he repeatedly makes the sign of the cross on the person's head and chest. The exorcist repeats this process until the demons have departed.

This is followed by reciting the Canticle of the Blessed Virgin Mary or the Canticle of Zechariah, the Athanasian Creed, and several other psalms, then concludes with a prayer asking God to keep the victim safe from the evil spirit.

The *third Chapter* gives instructions for ridding places of evil spirits, which begins with the long version of the prayer to St. Michael the Archangel, other prayers, an exorcism, a final prayer, and the sprinkling of holy water.

As is the case with the exorcism of a person, a priest must be authorized by his bishop to exorcise a place.

> When used by those who are authorized to do so, these prayers are extremely powerful.

Father Fortea states that "in 95 percent of possession cases, the demon shows himself after a few seconds of prayer."[284]

However, exorcisms are rarely resolved in just one session. "...[C]ommonly, they go on for six months to two years, and severe cases usually go on for a decade or more," explains Adam Blai. "Exorcism is a long process of disentangling the various lies and manipulations that they have instilled in their victim, casting out many demons over time. Eventually, the demonic manager of the case comes when all the lesser demons are removed, and in rare cases Satan comes to fight for the case after all other demons are expelled."[285]

Once a person has been liberated, they are encouraged to fully embrace the faith, usually beginning with confession and renewal of baptismal promises and the establishment of a solid and prayerful sacramental life.

---

284 *Interview with an Exorcist*, pg. 81
285 *Possession, Exorcism, and Hauntings*, pg. 63

If this is done, complete recovery is possible.

"In my experience, once a person is released – at times, after years of exorcism and prayers and not a few moments of discomfort – he usually does not have any permanent effects: he returns to his daily life, his relationships, and his work in a normal way," writes Father Amorth. "Indeed, he often understands that his new situation is a true and proper gift from God, asked for with insistence and at the end obtained. After this experience, he develops a sense of gratitude toward Jesus, toward our Lady, and toward the saints; his faith is stronger than ever."[286]

God's mercy never looks so glorious than it does to a soul who has been liberated from the very jaws of hell.

---

[286] *An Exorcist Explains the Demonic*, pg. 83

Chapter Five

How to Combat Satan

"The decisive defense is grace. These days we see a decline in reception of the sacraments, especially penance. This leaves us in grave danger, because we no longer have sufficient grace to forestall the invader who besieges us."

– Pope St. Paul VI

After reading the preceding chapters, it is obvious that the devil is to be feared. However, there is a right and a wrong way to fear him, a distinction which is critical to understand if we are to succeed in routing this deadly foe.

As Father P. Marie-Eugene writes, "The first condition for triumphing over the devil is not to give in to excessive fear. Assuredly, he is an enemy to be dreaded by reason of his power in the domain of sense and his cleverness; but we must not forget this deficiencies, his ignorance of the supernatural world, his powerlessness to penetrate into the higher faculties of our soul, and his status as a reprobate, which allows him only temporary victories and leaves him eternally conquered."[287]

In other words, our fear need not be a morbid one but must be well-informed in order to inspire within us a healthy respect for his exceptional prowess in view of his serious deficiencies.

---
287 *I Want to See God*, pg. 113

"To let oneself be overcome by terror of him would be as unreasonable as dangerous," Father continues. "The devil cleverly has recourse to this wile to conceal his own inferiority and to lay his snares. It would be to lose our advantages and increase his power and chances of success, to fear him beyond measure."[288]

In spite of having been frequently tormented by demons, St. Teresa of Avila exhorts the faithful not to be afraid of these diabolical forces and to ignore the horrors they present to us. "... [E]very time we pay little heed to them, they lose much of their power and the soul gains much more control over them...for their strength is nothing unless they find souls surrendering to them and growing cowardly, in which case they do indeed show their power."[289]

We have good reason to take her advice because in addition to teaching us about the reality of evil, our faith also give us confidence "by assuring us that the power of Satan cannot go beyond the limits set by God. Faith likewise assures us that even though the devil is able to tempt us, he cannot force our consent. Above all, faith opens the heart to prayer, in which it finds its victory and its crown. It thus enables us to triumph over evil through the power of God."[290]

As formidable as our enemy might seem, even more fearsome is our collection of weapons which are especially designed for combat with Satan. The first and most important of these weapons is being in the state of grace.

When asked how the faithful are to defend themselves against Satan, Pope St. Paul VI gave an unequivocal answer: "The decisive defense is grace." He went on to admit that even though this answer is an easy one to give, it is difficult to put into action, but the bottom line is the same: "All that defends us from sin protects us against the invisible enemy at the same time."[291]

---
288 Ibid
289 *The Life of Teresa of Jesus*, translated by E. Allison Peers, (Garden City, NY: *Image Books*, 1944) pg. 207-8
290 *Christian Faith and Demonology*, pg. 41
291 Pope St. Paul VI, General Audience, November 15, 1972

What is that defense?

Grace.

"Grace is favor, the free and undeserved help that God gives us to respond to his call to become children of God, adoptive sons, partakers of the divine nature and of eternal life," the *Catechism* teaches. "Grace is a participation in the life of God."[292]

The last thing Satan wants is to come up against a person who is surrendered to the Almighty. This is because they become like a Trojan Horse, seemingly small and inconsequential on the outside but with an interior life that is fully surrendered to the will of God and thus brimming with enough of His grace and power to vanquish him.

As Father Delaporte puts it, "Before a spirit man is like a child before a giant. Divine assistance alone restores the equilibrium."[293]

Being in a state of grace is a deal breaker for Satan. He may prowl around and perhaps land a blow or two, but the soul in a state of grace will only suffer superficially.

"Man in the state of grace is beloved by God; he is united to Jesus Christ, as the branch is to the trunk that nourishes it with its sap: in his soul, the Father, the Son, and the Holy Ghost do dwell, lending him a habitual and uninterrupted aid."[294]

However, when man sins and leaves the state of grace, God withdraws this crucial assistance and a person becomes vulnerable to the attacks of Satan. This is why it is so important that Christians refrain from all sin and be willing to make whatever life changes are necessary in order to conform their lives to the Commandments of God.

---

292 *Catechism*, No. 1996, 1997
293 *The Devil*, pg. 141
294 *The Devil,* pg. 150

"Good intentions are worth nothing," warns the exorcist, Father Fortea. "The law of God is objective, and must be obeyed."[295]

The decision to live a Godly life is up to each one of us. Although it may be difficult in some ways in our secular and highly relativistic society, the benefits reaped by remaining in close friendship with God protects us from the destructive power of Satan and are well worth the effort. However, we must be careful to develop these good spiritual habits primarily because we want to remain close to God – not just because we want protection from Satan.

"The primary purpose of all spirituality is growth in holiness, or greater union with God. Resisting the attacks of demons is a secondary effect. Another way to look at it is this: the closer we are to God, the safer we are from succumbing to demonic influence. It is important to keep our focus on God, not on the devil."[296]

How does the Christian go about insuring that they are in a state of grace? Although only God knows for sure who is – and who is not – in a state of grace, there are several things we are urged to do in order to acquire this state: attend the Sacraments of Reconciliation and Eucharist regularly, refrain from mortal sin as well as all attachment to sin, and stay close to God through daily prayer.

Sacramental Life

The sacraments are the most powerful channels for receiving grace, which is participation in the life of Christ, and are the best defense we have against demons.

Baptism is the first sacrament we receive. It wipes away original sin, makes us children of God, temples of the Holy Spirit,

---

295 *Interview with an Exorcist*, pg. 108
296 *Demons, Deliverance, and Discernment*, pg. 151

and brings us into the family of the Church. This sacrament affords us our first protection against the influence of demons.

The Sacrament of *Confession* is a powerful channel for receiving grace because it is the means by which our mortal sins are forgiven. These are the sins that open the door for demonic assault. This sacrament also gives us the strength to resist committing those sins again in the future.

As St. John Paul II explains: "The sacramental formula, 'I absolve you'…and the imposition of the hand and the sign of the Cross made over the penitent show that at this moment the contrite and converted sinner comes into contact with the power and mercy of God. It is the moment at which, in response to the penitent, the Trinity becomes present in order to blot out sin and restore innocence…God alone can forgive."[297]

The moment of absolution draws down all of the merciful power of God and sends the devil running for cover.

"…[C]onfession involves recognizing that God is the supreme lawgiver; admitting that we have disobeyed his laws, and being forgiven by him," writes Father Mike Driscoll. "These are experiences that the demons cannot and will not ever have. They refuse to recognize God's authority, and cannot admit that they are wrong. They will never experience the wonder of being forgiven, and hate the fact that we can."[298]

It's also important to note that "exorcism only drives a demon from one's body; confession drives out evil from one's soul."[299]

Church leaders such as Monsignor John Esseff, who served as one of St. Teresa of Calcutta's spiritual directors, once said that "One confession is worth a hundred exorcisms" because

---

[297] St. John Paul II, Apostolic Exhortation, *Reconciliatio et Poenitentia*, December 2, 1984, 31, III
[298] *Demons, Deliverance and Discernment*, pg. 151
[299] *Interview with an Exorcist*, pg. 70

of how this sacrament breathes life and divine protection into the soul.[300]

Father Amorth teaches that confession is "the most direct means to fight Satan, because it is the sacrament that tears souls from the demon's grasp, strengthens against sin, unites us more closely to God, and helps to conform our souls increasingly to the divine will."[301]

To those who are victims of demonic activity, he advises weekly confession.

Once forgiven of mortal sin and restored to the state of grace, the faithful are now free to receive nourishment from the *Eucharist*, also known as the *Bread of the Strong,* which is considered to be "the principal and indispensable weapon of the Christian in his spiritual combats with the infernal powers…"[302]

The reason so many Christians do not enjoy this treasure trove of grace is because they are not in a state of grace and either neglect to receive the Eucharist or receive it unworthily.

"In the Eucharist, we receive the true body, blood, soul, and divinity of Christ. Furthermore, we experience union with Christ and growth in his love as a special sacramental grace. Given that the demons are separated from God forever, are incapable of love, and are filled with hatred of God and all his creatures, it is no wonder that the love of Christ we receive in the Eucharist is so powerful against their work."[303]

Indeed, as Father Francis Fernandez teaches, when we receive Christ in the Eucharist, His divinity acts upon our soul with a far greater intensity than when He lived here on earth. "None of the people who were cured – Bartimaeus, or the paralyzed man

---

300 Armstrong, Patti Maguire, "Exorcist Warns Witches that Casting Spells Will Come Back to Haunt Them," *National Catholic Register,* July 14, 2017
301 *An Exorcist: More Stories,* pg. 195
302 *The Devil,* pg. 154
303 *Demons, Deliverance, and Discernment,* pg. 151

of Capernaum, or the lepers – were as close to Christ, to Christ himself, as we are every time we go to Holy Communion."[304]

This explains why St. Thomas Aquinas taught that the Eucharist "repels all the assaults of demons …. Like lions breathing forth fire, thus do we depart from that table, being made terrible to the devil."[305]

The Christian who worthily receives the Lord in the Eucharist "marches to battle clothed not only with the armor furnished by Jesus Christ, but with Jesus Christ Himself!"[306]

Prayer and Fasting

This weapon was given to us by the Master Himself when the disciples were unable to cast out a demon who was tormenting a boy. After chiding them as a "faithless generation" he told the boy's father, "This kind cannot come out by any way but *prayer and fasting.*"[307]

Prayer is fueled by faith. "Everything is possible to one who has faith,"[308] Jesus said. When prayer is backed by a strong faith, it becomes a mighty weapon in the hand of the believer.

"Faith lifts the soul above the domain of the senses, over which the devil can exercise power, and introduces it into the supernatural world, into which he cannot enter," Father P. Marie-Eugene writes. "Here then, the soul is inaccessible to its enemy; and consequently safe from his attacks and blows."[309]

To be vigilant in prayer is an indispensable weapon against the devil. This is why the Church has given us special prayers aimed at combatting infernal powers such as the prayers

---
304 Fernandez, Father Francis, *In Conversation with God, Volume Two* (London, UK: *Scepter,* 2015) pg. 426
305 *Summa Theologica,* I, 64, 4.
306 *The Devil,* pg. 155
307 Mark 9:29
308 Ibid, 9:23
309 *I Want to See God,* pg. 118

of exorcism and the prayer to St. Michael the Archangel; but we must be consistent in prayer and resist the temptation to quit if we don't see the results as quickly as we'd like. An inconsistent prayer life is not the way to ward off Satan who is always on the prowl, waiting for the right time to strike.

"As on exorcist said in regard to demonic possession, 'It's gradual steps. No one wakes up one morning [saying], *I'm possessed.* This has all taken place over an evolution of a relationship. By maintaining our daily relationship with Jesus Christ, we simultaneously avoid building a relationship with the devil."

We should also develop the habit of "praying constantly," as St. Paul admonishes us in 1 Thessalonians 5:17. This doesn't mean that we spend the whole day praying; it means that we "touch base" with God throughout the day and share with Him the daily ups and downs of our lives.

Father Amorth spoke about the power of prayer when he said that "we can be liberated from the demon with prayer alone, without any exorcism, but never with exorcism alone."[310]

This prayer must be sincere and from the heart. "Some people think specific – and repeated – prayers are needed for protection against the devil, but this is to think of prayer in 'magical' terms. Strictly speaking, it is not a particular prayer that protects us but the action of God Himself."[311]

Fasting is yet another indispensable weapon in our arsenal against the Evil One.

"It seems normal that the mortification of the senses, on which the demons ordinarily act, should first free us from their influence," Father P. Marie-Eugene writes. "By making us dominate nature, such mortification renders us like the angels and thus confers on us a certain power over the fallen angels."

---

310 *An Exorcist: More Stories*, pg. 191
311 *Interview with an Exorcist*, pg. 67

The lives of the saints are filled with details about holy men and women who courageously suffered harsh penances in expiation for their sins and for the conversion of sinners.

However, the Christian must be careful to exercise prudence in regard to these kinds of mortifications. This is because one of the ways Satan trips up the devout is to appeal to the last vestiges of their pride and encourage them to attempt severe penitential practices of which they might become boastful or seek to draw attention to themselves.

The best forms of penitential fasting are those that are similar to what the Church prescribes for Ash Wednesday and Good Friday, which consists of one full meatless meal and two small meals that together do not equal one full meal. Anything stricter than this should be under the advice of a spiritual director.

When practiced with humility and love, it is easy to see why fasting can be such a powerful weapon in the hand of the believer. As Father Fernandez explains, "The man who fasts turns toward God in an attitude of total dependence and abandonment. In Holy Scripture we see how fasting and other works of penance were performed before the commencement of any difficult task, to implore forgiveness for sin, to obtain the cessation of a calamity, to gain the grace needed for fulfillment of a mission, to prepare oneself to come face to face with God, etc."[312] as well as to uncover and repel the machinations of Satan.

Recourse to the Blessed Virgin Mary

Next to Jesus Christ, there is no more formidable enemy of Satan than the Blessed Virgin Mary. It is to her that God gave the assignment of defeating the primordial serpent when He decreed: "I will put enmity between thee and the woman and thy seed and her seed; she shall crush thy head and thou shalt lie in wait for her heel."[313]

---

312 *In Conversation with God*, pg. 43
313 Genesis 3:15

As St. Louis de Montfort explains, this enmity between the Evil One and Mary is irreconcilable.

"The most terrible of all the enemies which God has set up against the devil is His holy Mother Mary. He has inspired her...with so much hatred against that cursed enemy of God, with so much ingenuity in unveiling the malice of that ancient serpent, with so much power to conquer, to overthrow and to crush that proud, impious rebel, that he fears her not only more than all angels and men, but in a sense more than God Himself. Not that the anger, hatred and the power of God are not infinitely greater than those of the Blessed Virgin, for the perfections of Mary are limited; but first, because Satan, being proud, suffers infinitely more from being beaten and punished by a little and humble handmaid of God, and her humility humbles him more than the divine power; and secondly, because God has given Mary such great power against the devils that – as they have often been obliged to confess, in spite of themselves, by the mouths of the possessed – they fear one of her sighs for a soul more than the prayers of all the saints, and one of her threats against them more than all other torments."[314]

Mary's power over demons has been chronicled over and over again in the history of the Church and by numerous exorcists who claim that it was the Virgin who was the decisive factor in freeing their most difficult cases.

For example, Father Amorth describes an incident during an exorcism with his mentor, Father Candido, when the devil was asked why he was more afraid when the priests invoked Mary than when they implored God Himself. The devil replied, "I feel more humiliated being conquered by a simple creature than by God Himself."[315]

In another case, an exorcist had enough with the demon's stubbornness and turned to the altar of the Blessed Virgin and

---

[314] De Montfort, St. Louis-Marie, *True Devotion to Mary* (Rockford, IL: Tan Books, 2010) pg. 23
[315] *An Exorcist Explains the Demonic*, pg. 123

implored her to come to his aid. "...[O]ne little gesture from you, and the devil will go back to Hell." No sooner had he said this than the once-arrogant demon began to stammer and whine, "Madam, Madam...I am frightened, Madam...We can't say anything to you, Great Lady! It is forbidden to us...I shall have to go! I shall have to! Yes, Madam." The possessed woman was then relieved of her torments.[316]

Father Berger-Berges, an exorcist of long-standing, documented the same reaction to the presence of Our Lady in an exorcism, and added that "Never, never, has Satan been known to insult the Blessed Virgin Mary."[317]

In fact, one glance from her was enough to silence the demons who were causing a commotion during one of the apparitions in the grotto of Lourdes. According to Bernadette, the "young girl in white" had only to turn her eyes for a moment to the place where the noise was emanating, "and her one look was so effective, so endowed with sovereign authority, that the voices immediately fell silent."[318]

This explains why the Blessed Mother is invoked during the rite of exorcism. Although it is always God who liberates a person from the influence of Satan, "His ear is especially attuned to the mediation of Mary, the Mother of His Son."[319]

The Rosary is an especially powerful weapon against Satan which is why exorcists recommend this prayer to those who are being tormented by demons.

"This prayer has...a strong power of protection and liberation from evil," said Father Amorth. "One day Sister Lucia, a seer of Fatima, revealed that God has conferred a power so great on the Rosary that there is no evil – personal, family, or social – that cannot be defeated by its recitation with faith."[320]

---

316 *Angels and Devils*, pg. 260
317 Ibid
318 *Evidence of Satan in the World*, pg. 41
319 *An Exorcist Explains the Demonic*, pg. 123
320 Ibid

Intercession of the Saints

In addition to Mary, the faithful can tap into an enormous army of fellow warriors, known as the Communion of Saints, who have gone before us in the battle. In fact, the invocation of the Litany of the Saints is an important part of the rite of exorcism.

"For one who is troubled by a demon, the invocation of the saints during the rite of exorcism manifests this trust of the Church in their [the saints] presence," says Father Amorth.

"With those who enjoy the vision of God in paradise, an intense exchange of spiritual benefits takes place. Because of their more intimate union with Christ, the inhabitants of heaven do not cease to intercede for us with the Father, offering Him the merits they acquired on earth through Jesus Christ. Thus, our weakness is greatly helped by their fraternal solicitude."[321]

In his work, Father Amorth frequently felt the powerful presence of St. Pio of Pietrelcina, St. Catherine of Bologna, and St. John Paul II. "Of this last, I know for certain that he personally practiced at least three exorcisms in his private chapel in the Vatican. When I pronounce his name, the demons are literally infuriated."[322]

So powerful is the intercession of the saints that demons are loath to even mention their names directly.

"If they must mention them, they use substitutions. Jesus is referred to in reference to the priest who is performing the exorcism, such as 'your leader' or 'your superior'; Our Lady is 'that one there' or 'the thief of souls'; the saints are 'assassins.' They oppose [the saints] because, by their prayers, [the saints] steal souls from [the demons' claws]."[323]

This explains why demons are particularly repulsed by the relics of the saints. "...[R]elics of the saints torment demons

---

[321] *An Exorcist Explains the Demonic*, pg. 125
[322] Ibid, pg. 126
[323] Ibid, pg. 127

because they are filled with the spiritual anointing of these saints and call to mind the life of heroic sanctity the particular saint lived."

It's also important to note that in addition to helping us in our battle against Satan, the saints also teach us how to avoid confrontation, having learned that it's always best to evade engagement when possible.

As Father P. Marie-Eugene explains, the weapons with which the Church arms us are powerful indeed, and insure us of victory, "but the saints seem not to desire this struggle and do not seek it," he writes.[324]

Using the analogy of the traveler who is crossing a desert full of bandits, the traveler is prepared for these foes but doesn't seek them out even if he is assured of being able to defeat them. Instead, the traveler keeps his eyes on reaching the end of his journey.

"Neither does the soul *en route* to its God seek out the demons that might stop it, or at least retard it in its progress by causing it injuries. It stays out of their way. An excellent strategy is that of flight which shelters the soul from the attacks, the blows, and the tricks of the devil."[325]

It is a good habit to read the lives of the saints and learn from them the best tactics to employ in our battle against evil.

Sacramentals

The well-armed Christian will also avail himself of a variety of powerful sacramentals in the battle against evil.

As the *Catechism* explains: "These are sacred signs which bear a resemblance to the sacraments. They signify effects, particularly of a spiritual nature, which are obtained through the intercession of the Church. By them men are disposed to receive

---

324 *I Want to See God,* pg. 117
325 Ibid

the chief effect of the sacraments, and various occasions in life are rendered holy."³²⁶

A sacramental does not confer the grace in the same way that the sacraments do, but they prepare one to receive grace and dispose a person to cooperate with it.

There are three types of sacramentals – blessings, consecrations/dedications, and exorcism.

"Among sacramentals *blessings* (of person, meals, objects, and places) come first. Every blessing praises God and prays for his gifts. In Christ, Christians are blessed by God the Father 'with every spiritual blessing.' This is why the Church imparts blessings by invoking the name of Jesus, usually while making the holy sign of the cross of Christ."³²⁷

Another example of this type of sacramental is Holy Water. During the blessing of water, the Church "asks insistently that power be given to this water 'to put to flight all power of the enemy, to expel this enemy with all the rebels angels, to drive it away, to destroy the influence of the evil spirit and to cast out the venomous serpent.'"³²⁸

It is this blessing that gives the water its power. As Father Fortea explains, "...[A] material object – holy water, holy chrism, etc. – can torment or expel demons because the Church, with the power she has received from Christ, has given a special power to this object by blessing it. Of course, the object itself has no power; rather the power lies in that of Christ Himself which has been placed upon the particular object."³²⁹

Holy water should be in every home and used liberally. It is also a good practice to sprinkle the various rooms of the house with holy water and ask God's blessing upon one's residence.

---

326 *Catechism of the Catholic Church*, No. 1667
327 Ibid, No. 1671
328 *I Want to See God*, pg. 116
329 *Interview with an Exorcist*, pg. 66

Blessed crucifixes are another example of a sacramental that greatly disturbs the devil.

"It torments the demons because it reminds them of their defeat by Jesus' death on the Cross, of the final triumph of Christ over evil and death, and of their ultimate condemnation at the Last Judgment."[330]

Another type of sacramental is that of the *consecration or dedication* of a person to God.

"Certain blessings have a lasting importance because they consecrate persons to God, or reserve objects and places for liturgical use."[331]

This blessing pertains to that which is bestowed on men and women during the rite of religious profession, or when the faithful undertake certain ministries in the Church such as lector, extraordinary minister, or catechist. The dedication of a church or altar, the blessing of holy oils or vessels, are also examples of this type of sacramental.

Last, the Rite of *Exorcism* is considered to be a sacramental.

"When the Church asks publicly and authoritatively in the name of Jesus Christ that a person or object be protected against the power of the Evil One and withdrawn from his dominion, it is called exorcism."[332]

The simple form of exorcism is performed during the celebration of Baptism while the major exorcism can be performed only by a priest with permission of the bishop.

As Adam Blai recommends: "The people should seek the blessing of the priest as often as is reasonable. Their home should be blessed, as well as their transportation. Blessed holy symbols should be in each room of the home. The people should wear

---

330 *Interview with an Exorcist,* pg. 67
331 *Catechism of the Catholic Church,* No. 1672
332 Ibid, No. 1673

blessed objects... People should also seek indulgences when the Church makes them available."[333]

Angelic Protection

As we learned in Chapter One of this study, angels possess enormous power. In addition to having a superhuman intelligence and strength, they move at the speed of thought and can communicate mind-to-mind. These powers are what make Satan and his legions so dangerous, but they are also what make the good angels, whose power has not been corrupted by a fall, all the more formidable.

"...[O]ne can affirm that the angels who remained faithful to God have a certain degree of power against ordinary temptations as well as extraordinary spiritual evils. Why? Because they are of the same nature as the devils, and they fight with the same spiritual arms."[334]

In other words, they are a much better match for the evil one than we are.

We all know the story of the magnificent archangel Michael who responded to Lucifer's rebellion with the famous "Who is like unto God" before tossing him out of heaven. A powerful intercessor against evil, St. Michael is depicted in the Book of Revelation as "...fighting against the dragon; and the dragon and his angels fought, but they were defeated and there was no longer any place for them in heaven."[335] This is the reason why St. Michael is depicted as thrusting a sword into the serpent.

"The name 'Archangel' is given only to Saint Michael, even though sacred tradition and the liturgy of the Church attribute the same title to Saint Gabriel and Saint Raphael," writes Father Parente. "Saint Michel has always been the warrior Angel,

---

333 *Possession, Exorcism, and Hauntings*, pg. 20-21
334 *An Exorcist Explains the Demonic*, pg. 128
335 Revelation 12:7-9

fighting first Satan and his demons from the beginning, then in the course of time, all the enemies of God's own people."[336]

It is Saint Michael whom we invoke in the well-known prayer composed by Pope Leo XIII after a vision in which he perceived the power of evil that was pitted against the Church.

However, we can, and should, have recourse to our Guardian angels as well as to all of the angels of the nine choirs in our fight against evil.

It has long been a teaching of the Church that each of us has been gifted with one of these celestial powers who we refer to as our Guardian Angels.

"From the celebrated saying of Our Lord Jesus Christ, declaring that even little children have, to protect them, angels who see the face of the Heavenly Father, holy doctors and theologians have deduced, by plain reasoning, the belief in the Guardian Angel," writes Father Delaporte. "It is probable enough that each of us is more particularly attacked by one devil, as we are each specially guarded by one faithful spirit."[337]

The Guardian Angel is tasked with warding off dangers to body and soul; preventing the suggestions of Satan; removing occasions of sin and helping us to overcome temptation; enlightening and inspiring us with holy thoughts; offering our prayers to God and interceding for us; helping us at the moment of death; and conducting our souls to heaven or consoling us in purgatory.

"Although they cannot penetrate the inner sanctuary of human hearts which God has reserved for Himself, they do all they can to help us. However, it is in our power by an act of our free will to expose our intimate thoughts to our angelic

---

336 *The Angels*, page 92
337 *The Devil*, pg. 164

companion. And it is to our advantage for such confidence in his enlightened guidance is of great benefit to our soul."[338]

The spiritual masters urge the faithful to develop a strong relationship with their guardian angel and to rely upon them for help.

"Prayer to one's guardian angel is certainly efficacious: he has been given the mission to protect us; and against whom would he protect us if not against the fallen angels whom he can oppose with powers of his angelic nature and of the supernatural order."[339]

These mighty and magnificent guardians are a gratuitous gift given to us by a Father who loves us and wants to keep us safe from the evil that surrounds us.

"Just as fathers, when their sons have to travel among bad and dangerous roads, make sure they are accompanied by people who can guard them and defend them from dangers, so in the same way does our heavenly Father, as we set out along this path that leads to our heavenly home. He gives each one of us an angel," we read in the *Catechism of the Council of Trent*. "He does this so that, strengthened by his power and help, we may be freed from the snares cunningly set by our enemies, and may repel the terrible assaults that they make on us. He wants us to walk straight along the path with such guides, so that no obstacle placed in our way by the enemy should turn us aside from the way that leads to heaven."[340]

---

338 *St. Michael and the Angels* (Rockford, IL: *Tan Books and Publishers, Inc.*, 1983) pg. 33
339 *I Want to See God*, pg. 115
340 *Catechism of the Council of Trent*, IX, 4, quoted in *In Conversation with God*, pg. 69-70

Conclusion

> *"The apostle suggests the main line of defense:*
> *'Do not allow evil to win [but become all the more good]...*
> *win evil with goodness.'"*
> – Pope St. Paul VI

We have come to the end of our study and the enormous preternatural power and cunning of our Enemy should now be abundantly clear. He has an intellect so superior to man that we cannot even comprehend its capacity. He can influence our thoughts and trick us with his super-human cunning by laying a multitude of traps which are difficult to discern without the grace of God. A keen observer of man's behavior since the beginning of time, he knows exactly which buttons to push to tap into our individual psyches to discover and exploit our weaknesses.

However, as certain as we are of his great strengths, we are even more certain that he is outsmarted at every turn by the supernatural power of God and the many weapons He has provided to us. We must use those weapons and develop within ourselves the inner strength afforded by grace and growth in virtue.

Pope St. Paul VI told us on that fateful day in 1972, "Remember, the apostles listed the virtues that could make a Christian invincible and compared them to soldier's weapons. In his letter to the Ephesians, Saint Paul lists the inventory of the Roman weaponry; the helmet of salvation, the armor of the sword, and so on (Eph 6:13-17), to teach us that defense, to be effective, must be manifold. Being militant requires the Christian to be vigilant and strong; he must make use of special spiritual exercises if he wants to vanquish certain forms of diabolical attacks. Jesus himself teaches this truth to the apostles, when they are unable to cast out a demon: 'This kind cannot be driven out by anything but prayer and fasting' (Mk 9:29). Therefore, these are the means that we must use when we need to overcome some forms of diabolic attacks."[341]

It's up to each of us to pick up our weapons and fight.

St. John Henry Newman said it well: "You must either conquer the world or the world will conquer you. You must be either master or slave."

The Christian does not need tarot cards or psychics to know the future outcome of this primordial battle. We know from the Master Himself that we are already victorious in Him who has revealed the ultimate fate of the ruler of this world:

"I have told you this so that you may have peace in me. In the world you will have trouble, but take courage, I have conquered the world." [342]

---

[341] Quoted in *An Exorcist: More Stories,* pg. 71
[342] John 16:33

APPENDIX A

Protecting Oneself and the Home from Evil

The following recommendations are derived from a Pastoral Letter by the late Bishop Donald W. Montrose, bishop of Stockton, California, entitled, *Spiritual Warfare: The Occult Has Demonic Influence*:[343]

1. Confess all involvement in the occult – including any use of a Ouija board, tarot cards, psychic, astrology, etc. to a priest in the sacrament of Reconciliation.

2. Remove anything from the home that has had anything to do with witchcraft, a spiritualist, a medium, an oriental religion or cult or that has been used in a superstitious way. Destroy it or see to it that it is destroyed.

3. Do not keep jewelry that is symbolic of witchcraft or is a sign of the Zodiac.

4. Remove and burn all pornographic pictures and magazines—even those that have been put away in a drawer, closet or trunk.

5. Get rid of all religious literature that does not agree with the basic truth of our faith that Jesus Christ is divine. He is the Son of God, our only Savior who brings us to the Father. Remove

---

[343] Montrose, Bishop Donald W., *Spiritual Warfare: The Occult Has Demonic Influence*, accessed at Catholicebooks.com

and destroy literature from the Jehovah Witnesses, Mormons, Christian Science, Unity, Science of Mind, Scientology, Hare Krishna, Yoga, Transcendental Meditation, Divine Light Mission, Unification Church of Sun Myung Moon, the Children of God and the Way International. None of this or similar literature should be around our homes.

6. Do not allow the influence of evil to come into your home through television. Carefully monitor the programs that are seen. The values taught by television advertising are not the values preached by Our Lord Jesus Christ in the Gospel of St. Matthew, chapters 5, 6 and 7.

7. Keep blessed water in the home and use it frequently. If we wish to ask God's blessing on our own homes, we can say a simple prayer of blessing and then sprinkle holy water in each room. Such a prayer of blessing could be something like this:

   "Heavenly Father, we ask your blessing upon our home. In the name of your Son Jesus we ask to be delivered from sin and all evil influence. Protect us from sickness, accidents, theft and all domestic tragedies. We place our home under the Lordship of Jesus and consecrate ourselves to the Immaculate Heart of Mary. May all who live here receive your blessing of peace and love."

   An "Our Father" and "Hail Mary" could also be recited.

8. The consecration of the family and the home to the Sacred Heart of Jesus is another beautiful Catholic custom. We need to have a crucifix and pictures of the Sacred Heart and Our Blessed Lady in our homes.

9. Receive the Eucharist as often as possible. In this sacrament is the power and presence of Jesus Himself. Persons who have actually needed exorcism from the power of the Evil One have been cured by sitting in church in the presence of the Blessed Sacrament, an hour each day, for one or two months.

10. Pray to Our Lady, particularly the Rosary. Our Blessed Mother has been designated by God as the one who crushes the head of the serpent (Gen. 3:1). The Rosary is a very powerful means of protection and salvation. Many sons and daughters have been saved from the power of sin and the loss of faith through the perseverance of their parents in saying the Holy Rosary.

EFFICACIOUS PRAYERS

Prayer to St. Michael

St. Michael the Archangel, defend us in battle. Be our protection against the wickedness and snares of the devil. May God rebuke Him, we humbly pray, and do thou O Prince of the heavenly hosts, by the power of God, cast into hell Satan, and all the evil spirits, who prowl about the world seeking the ruin of souls. Amen.

Litany of the Saints

Lord, have mercy on us.
Christ, have mercy on us.
Lord, have mercy on us.
Christ, hear us.
Christ, graciously hear us.
God the Father of heaven, *have mercy on us.* (repeat after each line)
God the Son, Redeemer of the world,
God the Holy Ghost,
Holy Trinity, one God,
Holy Mary, *pray for us* (repeat after each line)
Holy Mother of God,
Holy Virgin of virgins,
St. Michael,
St. Gabriel,
St. Raphael,
All you holy angels and archangels,

All you holy orders of blessed spirits,
St. John the Baptist, *pray for us*
St. Joseph,
All you holy patriarchs and prophets,
St. Peter,
St. Paul,
St. Andrew,
St. James,
St. John,
St. Thomas,
St. James,
St. Philip,
St. Bartholomew,
St. Matthew,
St. Simon,
St. Thaddeus,
St. Matthias,
St. Barnabas,
St. Luke,
St. Mark,
All you holy apostles and evangelists,
All you holy disciples of our Lord,
All you holy innocents,
St. Stephen,
St. Lawrence,
St. Vincent,
Ss. Fabian and Sebastian,
Ss. John and Paul,
Ss. Cosmas and Damian,
Ss. Gervase and Protase,
All you holy Martyrs,
St. Sylvester,
St. Gregory,
St. Ambrose,
St. Augustine,
St. Jerome,
St. Martin,
St. Nicholas,

All you holy bishops and confessors,
All you holy doctors,
St. Anthony,
St. Benedict,
St. Bernard,
St. Dominic,
St. Francis,
All you holy priests and levites,
All you holy monks and hermits,
St. Mary Magdalen, *pray for us*
St. Agatha,
St. Lucy,
St. Agnes,
St. Cecilia,
St. Catherine,
St. Anastasia,
All you holy virgins and widows,
All you holy men and women, saints of God, *intercede for us.*
Be merciful, *spare us, O Lord.*
Be merciful, *graciously hear us, O Lord.*
From all evil, *deliver us, O Lord.* (repeat after each line)
From all sin,
From Thy wrath,
From a sudden and unprovided death,
From the deceits of the devil,
From anger, and hatred, and all ill-will,
From the spirit of fornication,
From lightning and tempest,
From the scourge of earthquakes,
From plague, famine and war,
From everlasting death,
By the mystery of Thy holy incarnation,
By Thy coming,
By Thy nativity,
By Thy baptism and holy fasting,
By Thy Cross and Passion,
By Thy Death and burial,
By Thy holy Resurrection,

By Thine admirable Ascension,
By the coming of the Holy Ghost, the Paraclete.
On the day of judgment.

We sinners, *we beseech Thee, hear us* (repeat after each line)
That Thou wouldst spare us,
That Thou wouldst pardon us,
That Thou wouldst bring us to true penance,
That Thou wouldst vouchsafe to govern and preserve Thy Holy Church,
That Thou wouldst vouchsafe to preserve our Apostolic Prelate, and all ecclesiastical orders in holy religion,
That Thou wouldst vouchsafe to humble the enemies of holy Church,
That Thou wouldst vouchsafe to give peace and true concord to Christian kings and princes,
That Thou wouldst vouchsafe to grant peace and unity to all Christian peoples,
That Thou wouldst vouchsafe to bring back to the unity of the Church all who have strayed away, and lead to the light of the Gospel all unbelievers,
That Thou wouldst vouchsafe to confirm and preserve us in Thy holy service,
That Thou wouldst lift up our minds to heavenly desires, *we beseech Thee, hear us*
That Thou wouldst render eternal blessings to all our benefactors,
That Thou wouldst deliver our souls, and the souls of our brethren, relatives, and benefactors from eternal damnation,
That Thou wouldst vouchsafe to give and preserve the fruits of the earth,
That Thou wouldst vouchsafe to grant eternal rest to all the faithful departed,
That Thou wouldst vouchsafe graciously to hear us, Son of God,

Lamb of God, who takest away the sins of the world, *spare us, O Lord.*
Lamb of God, who takest away the sins of the world, *graciously*

hear us, O Lord.
Lamb of God, who takest away the sins of the world, *have mercy on us.*

Christ, hear us.
Christ, graciously hear us.
Lord, have mercy on us.
Christ, have mercy on us.
Lord, have mercy on us.

Our Father, etc.
V. And lead us not into temptation
R. But deliver us from evil.

Ancient Prayers to the Blessed Virgin Mary

Sub Tuum Praesidium
(considered to be the most ancient prayer to Our Lady):

We fly to thy patronage, O holy Mother of God; despise not our petitions in our necessities, but deliver us always from all dangers, O glorious and blessed Virgin.

Memorare
(originated with St. Bernard of Clairvaux in the 12th century):

Remember, O most gracious Virgin Mary, that never was it known that anyone who fled to thy protection, implored thy help, or sought thy intercession was left unaided. Inspired with this confidence, I fly to thee, O Virgin of virgins, my Mother; to thee do I come; before thee I stand, sinful and sorrowful. O Mother of the Word Incarnate, despise not my petitions, but in thy mercy hear and answer me. Amen.

Consecration to Our Lady

O Eternal and Incarnate Wisdom! O sweetest and most adorable Jesus! True God and True Man, only Son of the Eternal Father, and of Mary ever Virgin! I adore Thee profoundly in the bosom and glory of Thy Father during eternity; and I adore Thee also in the virginal bosom of Mary, Thy most worthy Mother, in the time of Thine Incarnation.

I give Thee thanks, that Thou hast annihilated Thyself taking the form of a slave, in order to rescue me from the cruel slavery of the devil. I praise and glorify Thee, that Thou hast been pleased to submit Thyself to Mary, Thy holy Mother, in all things, in order to make me Thy faithful slave through her. But alas! Ungrateful and faithless as I have been, I have not kept the promises which I made so solemnly to Thee in my baptism; I have not fulfilled my obligations; I do not deserve to be called Thy child nor yet Thy slave; and as there is nothing in me which does not merit Thine anger and Thy repulse, I dare no more come by myself before Thy Most Holy and August Majesty. It is on this account that I have recourse to the Intercession of Thy most holy Mother, whom Thou hast given me for a Mediatrix with Thee. It is by her means that I hope to obtain of Thee contrition, and the pardon of my sins, the acquisition and the preservation of wisdom. I salute Thee, then, O Immaculate Mary living tabernacle of the Divinity, where the Eternal Wisdom willed to be hidden and to be adored by Angels and by men. I hail thee, O Queen of heaven and earth to whose empire everything is subject which is under God.

I salute Thee, O sure refuge of sinners, whose mercy fails no one. Hear the desires which I have of the Divine Wisdom; and for that end receive the vows and offerings which my lowness presents to thee. I, N. [Name], a faithless sinner, I renew and ratify to-day in thy hands the vows of my Baptism; I renounce for ever Satan, his pomps and works; and I give myself entirely to Jesus Christ, the Incarnate Wisdom, to carry my cross after Him all the days of my life, and to be more faithful to Him than I have ever been before.

In the presence of all the heavenly court I choose thee this day for my Mother and Mistress. I deliver and consecrate to thee as Thy slave, my body and soul, my goods, both interior and exterior, and even the value of all my good actions, past present and future; leaving to you the entire and full right of disposing of me, and of all that belongs to me, without exception, according to Thy good pleasure to the greatest glory of God, in time and in eternity.

Receive O gracious Virgin, this little offering of my slavery, in honour of, and in union with, that subjection which the Eternal Wisdom deigned to have to thy Maternity, in homage to the power which both of you have over this little worm and miserable sinner, and in thanksgiving for the privileges with which the Holy Trinity hath favoured thee. I protest, that I wish, henceforth, as thy true slave, to seek thy honour, and to obey thee in all things.

O admirable Mother, present me to thy Dear Son, as His eternal slave, so that as He hath redeemed me by thee, by thee He may receive me.

O Mother of mercy, get me the grace to obtain the true Wisdom of God, and for that end place me in the number of those whom thou lovest, whom thou teachest, whom thou leadest, and whom thou nourishest and protectest, as thy children and thy slaves.

O Faithful Virgin, make me in all things so perfect a disciple, imitator and slave of the Incarnate Wisdom, Jesus Christ thy Son, that I may attain, by thy intercession and by thy example, to the fullness of His age on earth, and of His glory in heaven. Amen.

(attributed to St. Louis de Montfort)

Prayer to St. Joseph, Terror of Demons

Courageous Joseph, advised by an angel, you confront your fears of the unknown. Your light shines brightly, penetrating the dark corners of your being. Your fears dispersed, you rediscover your true face, and actively participate in the divine project reuniting mother and Child, and the people with their God. Together with Mary and Jesus, you dwell in the love of God.

Help us to rediscover the united core of our identities, beyond all internal fears. Counsel us so we may build a better world to welcome the coming Kingdom. Shed your light on our inner lives that, freed from the grip of our fears, our decisions may be founded in Love. May the face of God shine on us![344]

Prayer to Our Guardian Angel

Heavenly father, Your infinite love for us has chosen a blessed angel in heaven and appointed him our guide during this earthly pilgrimage. Accept our thanks for so great a blessing. Grant that we may experience the assistance of our holy protector in all our necessities. And you, holy, loving angel and guide, watch over us with all the tenderness of your angelic heart. Keep us always on the way that leads to heaven, and cease not to pray for us until we have attained our final destiny, eternal salvation. Then we shall love you for all eternity. We shall praise and glorify you unceasingly for all the good you have done for us while here on earth. Especially be a faithful and watchful protector of our children. Take our place, and supply what may be wanting to us through human frailty, short-sightedness, or sinful neglect. Lighten, O you perfect servants of God, our heavy task. Guide our children, that they may become like unto Jesus, may imitate him faithfully, and persevere till they attain eternal life. Amen.[345]

Wearing of Blessed Objects

The Brown Scapular

Pope Benedict XV wrote: "Let all of you have a common language and a COMMON ARMOR: the language, the sentences of the Gospel; the common armor, the Scapular of the Virgin of Carmel, which you all ought to wear and which enjoys the singular privilege of protection even after death."[346]

---

344 Accessed on the website of St. Joseph's Oratory of Mount Royal, Montreal, Canada www.saint-joseph.org
345 Accessed on the Catholic News Agency website at www.catholic-newsagency.org
346 Davies, Father Peter O.Carm, "Our Lady's Brown Scapular: Sign of

The most ancient of all scapulars, the Brown Scapular was named by the Fathers of Vatican II as one of the most pre-eminent Marian devotions in the Church. Tradition dates the origin of the scapular to an apparition of Our Lady to St. Simon Stock on July 16, 1251. During the apparition, Our Lady made the promise: "Take this Scapular, it shall be a sign of salvation, a protection in danger and a pledge of peace. Whosoever dies wearing this Scapular shall not suffer eternal fire."

Although this pledge has sometimes been misinterpreted to mean that a person wearing the scapular can sin with impunity and still be saved, Our Lady's promise is to those who die while clothed in the scapular and to whom She will grant either the gift of perseverance in the state of grace or the grace of final contrition.

After being enrolled in the Scapular through investiture by a priest, the faithful agree to wear it always (a scapular medal can be substituted for those allergic to wool), and to fulfill certain conditions: recitation of some kind of daily Marian devotion such as the Rosary, or the Little Office of the Virgin Mary, and observing the chastity inherent in one's state of life.

Seventy-one years after the first apparition, Our Lady is said to have appeared to Pope John XXII and promised to favor those who wear her scapular with a speedy release from Purgatory, particularly on Saturdays. The emphasis on Saturday (in Latin, Sabbatum means Saturday) is why this second promise became known as the Sabbatine Privilege.

The words of the investiture blessing explain why this particular Scapular is so powerful against the machinations of evil: "May God Almighty, the Creator of Heaven and earth, bless you, He who has deigned to join you to the confraternity of the Blessed Virgin Of Mount Carmel; we beseech Her to crush the head of the ancient serpent so that you my enter into possession of your eternal heritage, through Christ our Lord."

Consecration to Mary," accessed at eCatholic2000.com

The Miraculous Medal

Given during an apparition to St. Catherine Labouré on November 27, 1830 at Rue de Bac, France, the front of this medal depicts Mary standing on a globe and crushing the serpent beneath her feet. The words "O Mary, conceived without sin, pray for us who have recourse to you," appeared in an oval around the figure. On the reverse, the medal bears a circle of twelve stars, a large letter "M" surmounted by a cross along with the Sacred Heart of Jesus crowned with thorns and the Immaculate Heart of Mary pierced by a sword. Our Lady asked St. Catherine to relate these images to her confessor and tell him that she wanted a medal made, promising that "All who wear it will receive great graces."[347]

The St. Benedict Medal

Although the exact date of the origin of the St. Benedict Medal is unknown, medals that bore the image of St. Benedict holding a cross aloft in his right hand and his *Rule for Monasteries* in the other hand have existed for centuries. These medals included a series of capital letters that were placed around the large figure of the cross on the reverse side of the medal. For a long time the meaning of these letters was unknown, but in 1647 a manuscript dating back to 1415 was found at the Abbey of Metten in Bavaria, giving an explanation of the letters. They are the initial letters of a Latin prayer of exorcism against Satan. These letters are included in the current version of the medal, which was struck in 1880 under supervision of the monks of Montecassino, Italy, to mark the 1400th anniversary of the birth of St. Benedict.

The Cross and C.S.P.B.: Crux mihi lux = On the back of the medal, the cross is dominant. On the arms of the cross are the initial letters of a rhythmic Latin prayer: *Crux sacra sit mihi lux! Nunquam draco sit mihi dux!* (May the holy cross be my light! May the dragon never be my guide!). In the angles of the cross,

---

[347] Glass, Joseph, "The Miraculous Medal," Catholic Encyclopedia

the letters C S P B stand for Crux Sancti Patris Benedicti (The cross of our holy father Benedict).

PAX (Peace) and letters around the outside edge: Above the cross is the word pax (peace), that has been a Benedictine motto for centuries. Around the margin of the back of the medal, the letters V R S N S M V - S M Q L I V B are the initial letters, as mentioned above, of a Latin prayer of exorcism against Satan: *Vade retro Satana! Nunquam suade mihi vana! Sunt mala quae libas. Ipse venena bibas!* (Begone Satan! Never tempt me with your vanities! What you offer me is evil. Drink the poison yourself!)

There is no special way prescribed for carrying or wearing the Medal of St. Benedict. It can be worn on a chain around the neck, attached to one's rosary, kept in one's pocket or purse, or placed in one's car or home. The medal is often put into the foundations of houses and building, on the walls of barns and sheds, or in one's place of business.

The purpose of using the medal in any of the above ways is to call down God's blessing and protection upon us, wherever we are, and upon our homes and possessions, especially through the intercession of St. Benedict. By the conscious and devout use of the medal, it becomes, as it were, a constant silent prayer and reminder to us of our dignity as followers of Christ.

The medal is a prayer of exorcism against Satan, a prayer for strength in time of temptation, a prayer for peace among ourselves and among the nations of the world, a prayer that the Cross of Christ be our light and guide, a prayer of firm rejection of all that is evil, a prayer of petition that we may with Christian courage "walk in God's ways, with the Gospel as our guide," as St. Benedict urges us.[348]

---

348 Courtesy of Father Isaac Haywiser, OSB

Use of Blessed (and/or Exorcised) Salt

Blessed salt, which is also considered to be a sacramental, can be used in much the same way as blessed water. The use of salt for religious purposes dates back thousands of years and is used to bless homes and can be used in the blessing of holy water. It is sometimes laid down in a line along the exterior perimeters of the house as a "line of defense" against the incursion of evil into the home.

An exorcism blessing can also be prayed over salt. According to the Roman Ritual, the priest prays: "O salt, creature of God, I exorcise you by the living God, by the true God, by the holy God, by the God who ordered you to be poured into the water by Elisha the prophet, so that its life-giving powers might be restored. I exorcise you so that you may become a means of salvation for believers, that you may bring health of soul and body to all who make use of you, and that you may put to flight and drive away from the places where you are sprinkled; every apparition, villainy, turn of devilish deceit, and every unclean spirit; adjured by him who will come to judge the living and the dead and the world by fire. Amen."

A similar blessing may be prayed over water by a priest: "O water, creature of God, I exorcise you in the name of God the Father Almighty, and in the name of Jesus Christ His Son, our Lord, and in the power of the Holy Spirit. I exorcise you so that you may put to flight all the power of the enemy, and be able to root out and supplant that enemy with his apostate angels, through the power of our Lord Jesus Christ, who will come to judge the living and the dead and the world by fire.

The priest will then pour exorcised salt into the water in the form of a cross and pray, "May the mixture of salt and water now be made, in the name of the Father, and of the Son, and of the Holy Spirit. Amen."[349]

---

349 Accessed at Romancatholicman.com

Epiphany Blessing

The annual Epiphany Blessing, which is a customary blessing that is bestowed on the home on the Feast of the Epiphany, is another powerful means of protection of the home. Conducted by either a priest or the laity, blessed salt is used to mark the front doorway with the initials of the three kings – C-M-B (Caspar, Melchior, Balthasar) – which also stands for the *Christus mansionem benedicat* "May God Bless This House." In a simple ritual that includes the reading of Scripture, the faithful mark the doorway(s) and then bless each room of the house with holy water while invoking the name of Jesus Christ.

How to Pray When Under Temptation

1. Pray until the temptation passes (pray to Jesus, Mary, the saints, your guardian angel, St. Michael, etc.)
2. Call upon the name of Jesus and/or Mary
3. Make the sign of the Cross
4. Proclaim Scripture
5. Bless yourself and sprinkle area with holy water
6. Don't let up until it passes

Seeking Freedom After Involvement in the Occult

In order to free oneself from any demonic influence as a result of occult activity, it is necessary to cease this practice, destroy all materials associated with it, and renounce, reject, and repent of this involvement through a simple prayer such as the following:

"Jesus, I repent of having been involved in (name activity). I reject and renounce this activity and ask for your forgiveness."

Seek absolution in the Sacrament of Reconciliation.

If negative influences continue, seek the counsel of a priest.

APPENDIX B

Bibliography

Alexander, Brooks, *Witchcraft Goes Mainstream* (Eugene, OR: *Harvest House Publishers*, 2004)

Amorth, Father Gabriele, *An Exorcist Tells His Story* (San Francisco, CA: *Ignatius Press*, 1999)

Amorth, Father Gabriele, *An Exorcist: More Stories* (San Francisco, CA: *Ignatius Press*, 2002)

Amorth, Fr. Gabriele with Stefano Stimamiglio, *An Exorcist Explains the Demonic: The Antics of Satan and His Army of Fallen Angels* (Manchester, NH: *Sophia Institute Press*, 2016)

Blai, Adam C., M.S., *Possession, Exorcism, and Hauntings* (2014)

Catechism of the Catholic Church (New York, NY: *Catholic Book Publishing Company*, 1994) No. 393

Congregation for the Doctrine of the Faith, *Christian Faith and Demonology* (Boston, MA:*Pauline Books & Media*)

Christiani, Leon, *Evidence of Satan in the Modern World* (Rockford, IL: *Tan Books and Publishers, Inc.*, 1961)

Congregation for the Doctrine of the Faith, *On the Current Norms Governing Exorcism*, September 29, 1985

Corte, Nicholas, *Who is the Devil?* (Manchester, NH: *Sophia Institute Press*, 2013)

Cruz, Joan Carroll, *Angels & Devils* (Charlotte, NC: *Tan Books & Publishers*, 1999)

Delaporte, Rev. Father of the Society of Mary, *The Devil: Does He Exist and What Does He Do?* (Rockford, IL: *Tan Books and Publishers, Inc.*, 1982)

De Montfort, St. Louis-Marie, *True Devotion to Mary* (Rockford, IL: Tan Books, 2010)

Driscoll, Father Mike, *Demons, Deliverance and Discernment: Separating Fact from Fiction About the Spirit World* (El Cajun, CA: *Catholic Answers Press*, 2015)

Encyclopedia of Occultism and Parapsychology, accessed online

Fernandez, Father Francis, *In Conversation with God, Volume Two* (London, UK: *Scepter*, 2015)

Gesy, Father Lawrence J. *Today's Destructive Cults and Movements* (Huntington, IN: *Our Sunday Visitor*, 1993)

Grimoire Encyclopedia, accessed online

International Catholic Charismatic Renewal Services Doctrinal Commission, *Deliverance Ministry* (Vatican City: *ICCRS*, 2017)

John Paul II, Apostolic Exhortation, *Reconciliatio et Poenitentia*, December 2, 1984

Kreeft, Peter, *Angels (and Demons): What do we really know about them?* (San Francisco, CA: *Ignatius Press*, 1995)

Labriola, John, *Onward Catholic Soldier* (Luke 1:38 Publishing, 2008)

Martin, Walter, Rische, Jill Martin, Van Gorden, Kurt, *Kingdom of the Occult* (Nashville, TN: *Thomas Nelson*, 2008)

Michel, Father P.J., SJ, *Temptations: Where They Come From, What They Mean, and How to Defeat Them*, (Manchester, NH: *Sophia Institute Press*, 2016)

Montrose, Donald W., D.D. *Spiritual Warfare: The Occult Has Demonic Influence*, Pastoral Letter, (Washington, NJ, *AMI Press*)

Noonan, Moira, *Ransomed From Darkness* (El Sobrante, CA: *North Bay Books,* 2003)

O'Brien, Michael D., *Harry Potter and the Paganization of Culture*, (Rzeszow, Poland: *Fides et Traditio Press*, 2010)

P. Marie Eugene, OCD, *I Want to See God: A Practical Synthesis of Carmelite Spirituality, Volume 1* (Allen, TX: *Christian Classics*, 1953)

Parente, Fr. Pascal P., *The Angels: The Catholic Teaching on the Angels* (Rockford, IL: *Tan Books and Publishers*, Inc., 1961)

Peers, E. Alison *The Life of Teresa of Jesus*, (Garden City, NY: *Image Books*, 1944)

Pontifical Council for Culture and Pontifical Council for Interreligious Dialogue, *Jesus Christ the Bearer of the Water of Life: A Christian Reflection on the New Age*, 2003

Scanlon, Michael TOR, and Randall J. Cirner, *Deliverance from Evil Spirits: A Weapon for Spiritual Warfare* (Ann Arbor, MI: *Servant Books*, 1980)

Sheen, Rev. Fulton J., *Life of Christ* (Mansfield Centre, CT: *Martino Publishing*, 2016)

St. Michael and the Angels (Rockford, IL: *Tan Books and Publishers, Inc.*, 1983)

Thurston, Herbert S.J., *The Church and Spiritualism* (Fort Collins, CO: *Roman Catholic Books*, 1933)

About the Catholic Life Institute

The Catholic Life Institute, acting under the patronage of the Immaculate Heart of Mary and Our Lady of Mount Carmel, is a lay-run apostolate devoted to infusing the world with the truth and splendor of the Catholic mystical tradition as revealed by the Carmelite saints and Doctors of the Church.

The Institute was founded by members of the Immaculate Heart of Mary Chapter of Discalced Secular Carmelites from Willow Grove, Pennsylvania to introduce Carmelite spirituality and authentic Catholic contemplation to the faithful. Our programs include courses on Teresian prayer, the interior life, the Little Way of Spiritual Childhood as taught by St. Therese of Lisieux, and spiritual warfare.

Our programs are presented by Susan Brinkmann, OCDS, an award-winning Catholic journalist who serves as the Director of Communications and New Age research for Women of Grace. She is the author of several books and is a frequent guest on EWTN. Her areas of expertise are in Carmelite prayer and spirituality, the New Age, and the occult.

The Catholic Life Institute Press is our newest addition and is used to publish our workbooks and other publications. In addition to our own books, the Institute also provides a wide collection of Church-approved Catholic books at discounted prices.

Our courses, books, retreats, and seminars are faithful to the Magisterium and completely free of New Age components.

Visit www.catholiclifeinstitute.org for more information.

About Our Cover

Deacon Lawrence Klimecki, the creator of the icon on the cover of this book, explains the meaning behind this art:

"Saint Joseph is one of our most powerful intercessors. Here he is shown exemplifying three of his traditional titles. He stands before two priests, putting himself between the priesthood and any harm that comes to it. Joseph is the protector of priests as he was the protector of the one High Priest, Jesus. His obedience to the word of God conveyed to him by angels also serve as a model for priestly obedience. Joseph cradles a boat in his left arm. The ship (or bark/barquentine) is an ancient symbol of the Church. The Church carries the faithful across the stormy seas of the world. Saint Joseph was the head of the divine household, the first 'domestic Church.' As the guardian of the Holy Family in Nazareth, he now extends his protection over the entire Church of Jesus. Joseph stands upon the back of a demon which is shown defeated, face to the ground. As protector of the Holy Family, Joseph defended Mary and Jesus against threats visible and invisible. The invisible threats came from the spiritual world, demons who have turned away from God. Saint Joseph was surely endowed with graces that struck the demons with terror. The Litany of Saint Joseph describes him as such, the Terror of Demons."

Made in the USA
Middletown, DE
16 August 2020

15224440R00089